THE FALLACY OF THE ISLAMIC STATE

BADRELDIN YOUSIF ELSIMAT

CONTENTS

Introduction to the Second Edition

The Islamic State of Iraq and Syria (ISIS) a By-Product of Traditional Islamic Schools of Thought

The first edition of this book appeared in the Arabic language, few months before the unfortunate declaration of the establishment of the Islamic State of Iraq and Syria (ISIS). However, the writer was very alert and keen to point out the eminent danger and the potential catastrophic consequences accompanying the establishment of any Islamic state.

It was stated clearly in the first Arabic edition of this book, that a formation of an Islamic state under any name, however carefully promulgated, will lead to violation of fundamental human rights and ultimately to violence, bloodshed and butchery. It was neither a prophecy nor future telling, but a logical prediction supported and confirmed by an accurate and correct reading of Muslim traditional literature, as well as overwhelming historical evidence.

In this critical historical juncture, one cannot conceive a more blessed mission, a more noble cause or a more sacred human endeavor than the protection of freedom of thought and defense of fundamental human rights. Freedom is the mother of all virtues. However, many obstacles, innumerable forces, uncountable challenges, and the ignorance of centuries stand blocking the way towards human liberation and final redemption. Militant Islam, which politicises religion and uses the blessed name of Islam to achieve political ends, is the most direct and strongest of these diverse forces. Political Islam is a threat to liberty, freedom of thought, culture and civilisation. It is an organised threat humanity has never witnessed before. Throughout history, human liberty has always been in danger of perishing, but never has it been endangered on such a large scale as now.

During the last three decades, the world has witnessed dreadful violence and serious discriminatory policies of the Islamists, whether they seized power or not. Take for example the Shi'ite of Iran, the Taliban of Afghanistan, the Muslim Brothers of Sudan & Egypt and their offspring, Jammat Jihdiya wa Takifria and the Ansaar Bait Al-Maqdis; look at the Shabab Al Islam of Somalia, Hezbollah of Lebanon, Hamas of Gaza, Jema'ah Islamiya of Pakistan, Boko Harram of Nigeria, Abu Sayaf of Philippines, the Jihadists of Libya and Algeria, Dar Al Islam of Indonesia, Hutheen of Yemen, the Jabhat Nusra group, the Qaeda Organisation and last but not least, ISIS (Da'ish in Arabic). The brutal crimes of all these various groups have darkened the face of the globe and robbed the world of its security. The human conscience was shocked by the barbarous beheadings committed by ISIS in cold blood.

Denial of fundamental human rights is the common factor, which knits together Islamic groups in a strong interwoven bond, though they belong to different or even opposing schools of thought. They are separate organisations, and sometimes zealous individuals, yet they appear collective. Even the moderate Muslims of Turkey, Malaysia or Tunisia, or the so-called Islamic scholars, share the same erroneous way of thinking. The difference is only in degree not in kind. Moderate and fundamentalist Muslims are two sides of the same coin. The apparent difference rests in the temporary tactics and strategies dictated by rapid modernisation in all fields, grave political necessities and powerful social demands.

A host of Muslim scholars teaching Islamic jurisprudence, history and oriental studies in western universities issued a lengthy memorandum to distance themselves from ISIS. Muslim councils in the USA, Canada, European countries, and the Arab and Islamic world, struggled and exerted tremendous efforts to distance themselves from ISIS. Their efforts and struggle did not clear the dilemma or solve the problem. On the contrary, their efforts created puzzling and perplexing confusion in the minds of non-Muslims, as well as Muslims, thus leading to more violence and violations to the rule of law.

The significant and crucial questions, which were left unanswered by Muslim scholars and the rest of the Islamic world, are: From where did this confusion come into being? From where did this violence arise? What is the origin of all this chaos? Why does violence arise instantly and automatically whenever there is a call for an Islamic state? What is the relationship between Islam and violence?

These are legitimate questions, which should be asked by any serious individual who cares for the future of humanity. The answer to all these questions is simple and direct:

There is a close relationship between an Islamic state and violence, while there is no relationship between Islam and violence!

This answer may intrigue the reader and arouse their curiosity because it appears contradictory and puzzling. Yet this is not the case. Everything will become explicit and crystal clear when the reader understands that there is neither a political system in Islam nor a form of government. The Islamic state is a fallacy and an erroneous concept, which was introduced to Islam immediately after the passing away of Prophet Mohammed and his ascent to the glories of the Heavens, or rather, while the Prophet was at his deathbed.

The reader may be greatly astonished and taken by surprise to find in this book that the concept of the Islamic state is not supported by the Quran, which is the holy book of Islam and its ultimate and final authority. This statement is not the opinion of the writer, nor is one of his fancies or dreams. Rather, it is a fact supported by detailed analysis and classification of the Quranic verses, as revealed in this book. Moreover, references to the teachings and practices of Prophet Mohammed (the Sunnah) confirm what the writer is stating. Prophet Mohammed was neither a king nor a President of State. He defined himself as a messenger of God, and his companions strictly and respectfully adhered to this description all through the Prophet's time. Mohammed was never known or referred to otherwise. Mohammed was and still is affectionately called Rasoul Allah i.e. 'The Messenger of God'. Not only this, but the conduct of Prophet Mohammed and his two leading disciples (Ali & Abu Bakr) supports the writer's point of view and conviction. The reader will find full demonstrations and quotations proving such an allegation inside this book. After all, Islamic mysticism (Tasawuf), which is the heart of Islam, was based on separation of Islam from the state.

An Islamic state is a false idea. It is no wonder that mass killings and massacres occur whenever there is a call for an Islamic state. A false concept will never lead to the truth, in the same way that the bad will never lead to the good. The Islamic state is a baseless idea, supported by nothing but the power of the sword. The origin of the concept of the Islamic state can be traced to the great wars and bloody battles, which broke out between the companions of Mohammed in the early days of Islam. This pandemonium was nothing but a covetous search for power, wealth and prestige.

If the Islamic State is a fallacy, what is Islam then?

The literal meaning of the Arabic word Islam is 'to surrender', indicating the acceptance of the supreme will that governs all the cosmos. Peace is also an intrinsic component of the definition of the word 'Islam'. The confusion originated from the fact that the Holy Quran is word and spirit in one breath and at the same depth. As ancient wisdom tells us: the letter kills, only the spirit gives eternal life! That is if you stop at the literal meaning of the word, you will become completely unaware of the source and light behind the word. If you repeat the word 'cow' millions of times you will not get even an iota of milk, but one real living cow will give you plenty of milk. In the same way, if you repeat the word 'God' millions of times, it will lead you nowhere. However if the light of God strikes your heart even for a fraction of a second, you will reach a state of immortality and ever-lasting illumination. Prophet Mohammed was referring to those spiritual heights when he said: 'I have an hour with Allah where no Angel or Prophet dares to approach'; or when he said: 'A thoughtful hour is better than seventy years of worshiping God'.

The Quran tells Mohammed: *'Thus we have revealed to you the spirit of our order (highest order) as you were not aware of the meaning of the book or the meaning of belief... It is (book and belief) manifested as a light, through which we guide whom we ever wish)'* (Shoora: 52).

Therefore, the Quran is not only the word. The essence of the Quran is the spirit and the light of God. If one understands the Quran properly and lives accordingly, he will become a light unto himself, as clearly stated in the Quran: *'The human being is a light unto himself'* (Al-Quyama:14). The literal interpretation of words of the Quran is termed 'Tafseer'. The true meaning of the Quran and the light behind the words is the essence of the Quran, and is termed in Arabic 'Taweel'. Tafseer, or literal interpretation, leads to the erroneous concept of the Islamic state. Taweel means diving deep into the essence, and origin of the human self and the cosmos, and ultimately leads to Islamic mysticism (TASWUF) and to separation of Islam from the state, thus paving the way towards peace and love. This is the idea I was conveying by my previously mentioned statement: **'There is a close relationship between an Islamic state and violence, while there is no relationship between Islam and violence!'**

Islam between TAFSEER and TAWEEL

Islamic mysticism is based on understanding TAFSEER, and going beyond it towards TAWEEL.

TASWUF is based on separation of Islam from the state. After the assassination of Ali and his son Al-Hussein (the reader will find a narration of the whole story in the relevant chapters of this book), a grandson of Ali, named Ali Zain Al Abideen and many faithful Muslims concluded that their Muslim brothers had failed to understand their religion. Consequently, the Sufis chose to live in seclusion and abandoned the corrupt society. For them, it was best to isolate themselves. These great men, and sometimes women, started a process of self-purification called in Arabic Al–SULOOK. They attained profound spiritual experiences. Generally, they were knowledgeable, thoughtful, helpful, lovable people of good conscience and integrity of character. They were humble, modest and austere. They never acquired property or heaped wealth nor lived in grand palaces as did the Caliphs of the Omayyad and Abbasids. It is to be noted that the Omayyad and Abbasids ruled the Islamic world for the first six hundred years of the advent of Islam i.e. from 661 until the Mongols conquered the Middle East in 1285.

Sufis preserved the spiritual side of Islamic culture and developed new concepts away from the tyranny of the Caliphs. They spread Islam through peaceful methods in India, Far East, and the Sudan. They preserved Islamic culture in Egypt, North and West Africa, Syria, Jordan, Lebanon, Iraq, Iran and Turkey. Although Islam spread by the power of the sword, Sufism was responsible for the preservation of Islam for over a thousand years. There are many other factors, which allowed for the spread of Islam, but Sufis were the pioneers.

Great Sufi leaders elevated the crude Islamic monotheism to the concepts of Oneness with God, and Oneness of Existence, which are termed respectively (WUSUL, and WAHDAT AL-WUGOOD in Arabic). Sufi literature is one of the most refined and polished literatures the world over, in form as well as substance. Great Sufi leaders were blessed with many faculties. They were eloquent and talented. Their visions were unfathomable. Their wonderful writings were beautified with sweet words, rosy expressions, picturesque descriptions of nature, and elegant poetry. Unparalleled abilities in metaphor and symbolism characterise the finest Sufi writings. There is a flame of truth in fine Sufi literature. One immediately feels the fire of illumination and the coolness of peace, in one breath. You may feel as if you are reading the heights of the Upanishads, the Vedas or the Gita of the Hindus. It is similar in some ways to the Nirvana of the Buddha, and Jesus's Sermon on the Mount.

In fact, Sufis embraced and shook hands with all religions, without discrimination. Most of the time they did not apply the rigid rules of Islamic law. They used symbolism to avoid the tyranny of the Caliphs, which caused them trouble with the then police state. Nevertheless, the Sufis succeeded in some ways to tame the rigidity of Islamic monotheism.

Al-Nabulsi, a great Syrian Sufi, said, addressing God in fine poetry:
'You are fantastically near to me,
Till I witnessed you are me.
But when I realised my situation, and state of mind
And illusions abandon me, and hide,
I left this and that...
And all things faded away
Then annihilation (al-fana)
Became my art, and my way'
Al-Nabulsi means to say that God is as near to him as the Quran says about Allah's proximity to man: *'We are nearer to man than the jugular vein'* (Quaf: 16).

Al-Nabulsi extended and elevated the Quranic meaning to witness the oneness of man and God. After realisation and extinction of illusion, he left behind both ideas, 'man' and 'God', and entered the Great Silence, the Great Void of Nothingness, which is analogous with the Hindu Muksha and Buddhist Nirvana.

Nabulsi also surpassed the crude idea of hell and paradise to unity with God himself. He reflected on the peaks of such heights, in elegant poetry. Nabulsi was not an alone voice. Many other like-minded Sufis were on the same wave-length. To name a few: Ibn Arabi, Al-Giali, Al-Genaid, Al –Shibly, Al-Bustami, Rumi, and Al-Halaj. The reader will find some details about these great masters in the relevant chapters of this book.

Unfortunately, many Sufi leaders who dared to address the public were crucified, assassinated or imprisoned. For this reason, some Sufis formed secret cults in order to talk safely to their disciples. Secrecy led to corruption, decay and deterioration of Sufism. Many clandestine cults grew under the blessed name of Sufism. Nevertheless, even in its pure form and pristine glory, Sufisim cannot satisfy the needs of modern humanity. Modern humanity is yearning for liberation from all conditioning and is aspiring for higher spiritual dimensions not trodden by our forefathers. Sufism cannot answer the complicated questions of our atomic age of Nano medicine, Higgs boson, human genome, new social and political dimensions, weapons of mass destruction, computer science, sophisticated communication devices and fast transport systems, which have made our globe shrink to a small village; all of these were beyond prediction. Sufism needs renewal and development. It needs to evolve.

However, in the twentieth century, the Muslim sage Mahmoud Mohammed Taha (affectionately called Ustadh in Arabic i.e. master) promulgated in the Sudan what he called the 'Second Message of Islam'. The Second Message of Islam blew a new breath into Sufism, and revived the true face of Islam.

Unfortunately, this great spiritual leader was executed for apostasy (ALRIDH) in Khartoum, Sudan on 18 January 1985. The leadership of his organisation fell to lesser hands. It goes without saying, and as was expected, the Ustadh faced death with a smile of contentment second to none. It is the normal bravery of leaders of his caliber since the times of Socrates and Jesus Christ. The writer published a book about Ustadh in Arabic titled 'Recalling the Days of Allah'.

The Muslim Brothers, who are currently ruling the Sudan disgracefully, promulgated in their Penal Code provisions for killing the apostate (AL MURTAD). The world is not likely to forget the story of the Sudanese girl Mariam Yahya Ibrahim Ishaq, who was recently convicted of apostasy, because of her Christian faith, and courageously faced the death sentence. Fortunately, Mariam's death sentence was lifted after huge international and Christian pressure on the government of Sudan.

The reader will find references given in this book to the spiritual, intellectual and cultural revolution of TAWEEL, as founded and initiated by the writer of this book. Separation of Islam from the state is based on TAWEEL. Although TAWEEL is not the subject of this book, it may be beneficial to the reader if she/he has access to the writer's books on TAWEEL published in Arabic and currently on their way to be translated into English under the following titles:

1.   Beyond Words, at the Shores of Eternity;

2.   The Fragrance of the Flower of Higher Life;

3.   Signs on an Untrodden Path;

4.   Recalling the Days of Allah;

5.   The Fallacy of the Islamic State;

6. New Approach to the Sudanese Crisis;

7. Imageries on the Margins of the Hearts, and the Advent of the Intellectual revelation;

8. Bridges over the Sea of the Timeless.

In addition, there are four other books, which will be published shortly.

The Military Option is not an Option, and War is the Shame of Mankind

As it appears from above, the rise of military Islam cannot be prevented by non-Muslims. Despite international commitment, investment of huge financial resources and high-tech military equipment, terrorism is on the rise. The root causes behind the attraction of the youths to terrorist groups have not been properly addressed. It is a naive approach to pretend that reforming educational systems, creating job opportunities for the youth, calling for peace campaigns and assisting governments to practice good governance will solve the problem. The crucial point is: Who will reform the educational system? Who is going to launch a peace campaign? Bearing in mind, that most Islamists are educated and trained in the West.

The root causes of Islamic terrorism are far deeper than such superficial analysis. Islamic terrorism is more dangerous than Nazism. During the early years of Hitler, intellectuals kept silent. They superficially assumed that Nazism was a new trend in politics, nationalist ideology and an isolated extremist project. The western world adopts the same mentality with the Islamists of Why bother? It is an internal problem of Muslim countries. It is an isolated extremist group. It is just a change in politics. Young people are oppressed by poverty, and are looking for change. People simply want to preserve their religion and integrity. They want to apply their traditional laws. So why bother?

Such a naive approach is extremely remote from the truth. Hitler was a victim of a strange obsession regarding the superiority of his race. His entire struggle was aimed at forcing the whole world under his leadership by the force of the gun, whatever the price might be. Similarly, Islamic fundamentalists are victims of a strange obsession regarding the superiority of their religion. The purpose of their entire struggle is to force the whole world under their leadership by the power of the gun.

The only difference with Nazism is that you have only one Hitler, but in the Islamic movements there are many Hitlers. Moreover, Islamic militants are more zealous, enthusiastic and ready to die for their cause. The reason is obvious. Tradition is more inspiring than nationalism in the battlefield, and is more deeply rooted in the human self. Beware. Since the world is fast asleep, it is easy for the Islamists to achieve their goals. In the past, the Muslims conquered all of Arabia, the Persian Empire, North Africa, Egypt and Spain within a few decades, and were knocking on the doors of Europe. They were defeated only at the boarders of France. The establishment of ISIS is solid proof that the Islamic movement is a threat to liberty, freedom of thought, culture and civilisation.

Only Muslims, through renewal of Islam, will be able to solve the dilemma and save the world. The USA and its Western allies committed a grave mistake by resorting to war and fighting violence with another form of violence. Modern destructive weapons have made war a disaster to the victorious as well as the defeated. In fact, all throughout history war has been a disaster. In the end, war never resolved any problem. On the contrary, humanity is trapped in a vicious cycle from war to truce to war again. War is nothing but organised butchery. It is the shame of mankind, a shame we did not fully experience and feel, because our sense of compassion is still crude and immature. Our egocentric minds do not feel the pain and agony of others - the widows, orphans and men who lost their lives, not to mention the growing number of displaced people and refugees. We only feel the pain when it hits us directly or it hits a loved one. Human suffering is immense, but we are not completely aware of the depth of it.

One cannot fight ISIS and militant Islam with the same violence. Violence and war of any form must be condemned and totally denounced, including defensive war. Western politicians are confused regarding the ISIS crisis. Of particular interest, is the evident contradiction between the so called moderate Muslims, and the extremist Muslims including ISIS militants. The former preach peace, love, freedom and equality, when quoting Quranic verses, while the latter preach violence, war, hatred, slavery and discrimination when quoting Quranic verses. This state of contradiction should be examined carefully and not just slurred over. This strange phenomenon has led to the confusion of Western scholars as well as the Western politicians. This perplexing result is exactly what the fundamentalists want. In the midst of this confusion, western politicians reached the wrong conclusion and have been dragged into a vicious, bloody and destructive war. Nobody yet knows the human and financial cost, the duration or the result of this ill-planned war.

It should be hopefully clear to the reader why there are apparently contradicting verses in the Quran. Only through proper understanding of the TAWEEL, will this oddity and contradiction be intelligently solved and finally removed.

Peace can only come through understanding of the oneness of existence and the oneness of the motherhood of mankind. No real peace is ever to come unless each individual touches this oneness and lives in harmony within himself. All exterior conflicts are reflections of interior individual conflicts. Unless one knows himself fully, comprehensively and deeply, peace will always remain a mirage. This is the subject of TAWEEL, the full explanation of which is beyond the scope of this book.

The ONLY Solution

Separation of Islam from the state paves the way to world peace. Historical records of the centuries during which Islamic law, (termed Sharia in Arabic) was the governing standard, indicate that human rights and fundamental freedoms were theoretically and practically non-existent. The Turkish Empire, the Fatimieen of Egypt, the Abbasids dynasty, the Omayyad dynasty are clear examples challenging whoever wishes to argue otherwise.

Sharia grossly discriminates against people on the basis of religion, creed and gender. In addition, slavery is a concept, which permeates Sharia. For example, the Islamic veil worn by women (Hijab), is not merely a piece of cloth. It is a symbol of seclusion, segregation and slavery for women. In Arabic female slaves are called: MA MALKAT AYMAKUM & JAWARI. But more generally, Islamic Jihad through the power of the sword will rob the world of its security and civilisation and will revive the institution of slavery. The Islamic Turkish Empire refused to illegalise and abolish the institution of slavery and the Omar Conventions. Omar Conventions (ALUHDA ALUMARIA in Arabic), were rules promulgated by Caliph Omar Ibn Al-Khattab in the first century of Islam to humiliate and discriminate against

Jews and Christians. Slavery and the Omar Conventions were only cancelled under heavy European pressure on Sultan Abdulmageed of Turkey in 1856. It is to be noted that no Islamic jurist criticised the institution of slavery all through Islamic history except in modern times, but such criticism is never genuine as had been indicated earlier.

Although democratic systems and liberal thought can be traced to ancient Athens before the advent of Christianity, human rights are a recent legal transplant. Since 1945, The Charter of the United Nations imposed on all member states the obligation: 'to achieve international cooperation in solving international problems of an economic, social, cultural or humanitarian character and in promoting and encouraging respect for human rights and fundamental freedoms for all without distinction as to race, sex, language, or religion'.

Wahabi groups and Muslim Brothers' ways of thought, which came to climax in militant Islamic movements, and culminated in the establishment of ISIS, had always been a challenge to democracy. The late Egyptian cleric Hassan Al-Bana, the founder of the Muslim Brotherhood Movement (1927) and the rest of the clerics belonging to similar traditional Muslim schools of thought, demonstrated contempt for liberty, disregard for others and advocated and used violence as a means to achieving political ends.

The rise of constitutional democracies and recognition of fundamental human rights are one of the greatest and most extraordinary achievements of all times. They did not enter into existence smoothly and gently. They were handed to us through untold sacrifices - sweat, tears and blood of our forbearers in their age-old relentless struggle and yearning for freedom. Even modern science is a legitimate child of human strife for liberation from the slavery of ancient theories and all sorts of illusory preconceived ideas.

Therefore, it is the sacred responsibility of everyone enjoying life and freedom on this planet to join all other enlightened individuals in order to rein in the horses of political and militant Islam. Such a feat can only be achieved through a new and creative understanding of Islam. It is the only way to up-root and eradicate ISIS, militant Islam, Muslim Brothers' ways of thought and all Muslim traditional schools; thus paving the way towards liberation and final human redemption.

Badreldin Yousif Elsimat / January 2015

Introduction to the First Edition

Since the departure of the great Prophet of Islam and his ascent to the heavens in 632 AD, his companions disagreed on matters of succession (Khilaapha)[1], state affairs and on the idea of a 'religious government'. This disagreement was terribly divisive and devastating. Rivers of blood were spilled over this dispute in the early years of Islam and throughout the days of the Righteous Caliphs[2]. In fact, this bloodshed for the purpose of Khilaapha and political power has continued relentlessly and mercilessly throughout Islamic history.

It is high time for Muslims, along with this bewildered planet, to stop, observe and realize that the concept of an Islamic or religious government is completely erroneous. It is a belief that has no support whatsoever in the Holy Quran or in the pure Sunnah of the Prophet.

---

1 'Khilaapha' is Arabic for succession. The word 'Caliph' is also used to mean 'head of the state'. Both words originate from the same root.

2 The term 'Righteous Caliphs' (also known as the 'Rashidun Caliphs') refers to Caliphs: Abu Bakr El-Sideeq, Omar Ibn Al-Khattab, Othman Ibn Affan and Ali Ibn Abi Talib.

Moreover, this belief in a 'religious government' is contradictory to modern constitutional principles, as well as the Universal Declaration of Human Rights. The pursuit of an erroneous concept, which contradicts human freedom and liberty, will inevitably lead to blood baths, massacres and gross atrocities. This has happened wherever and however the issue of an Islamic state has been raised. Throughout history, the idea of establishing a religious government has always been accompanied by the phenomenon of extreme violence. It is, however, particularly alarming in this modern time, in which all human beings are aspiring for truth, freedom and perfection. In one word, for peace.

This brief book sheds some light on this vital and important subject. The arguments are presented on the basis of the explicit text of the Holy Quran and the Sunnah. The reader will notice a striking consistency between the provisions of the scriptures and the insight of the writer. The reader will also be in a position to recognise a harmonious synchronicity of this insight with historically established facts.

The book will not only deal with questions relating to the method for selecting a 'Head of State', or a 'Caliph' for Muslims, but will go directly to the heart of the matter and explore the idea of an Islamic government/state itself. We will then see that the concept of an Islamic state is baseless in the Quran and in the Sunnah.

The subject of the religious government has always been considered taboo. Suppression of dialogue on the subject and the relevant question of 'obligatory allegiance', in addition to continuous terrorising of political opponents, have all led to either violent resistance and war by the strong, or to hypocrisy and helplessness by the weak. It is apparent that no good could come out of either attitude.

It is a heavy burden, which has dissipated precious time, breeding intolerance, stagnation and fossilisation, allowing for premature emotions to be provoked to galvanise milllons of Muslims, sending them blindly into vicious wars in order to kill their fellow humans in cold blood. Ristricting the great religion of Islam to lifeless formality has had detrimental effects on the development of Islamic thought. Islam has been reduced to a power struggle, which allows for religious decrees and covenants to be used for mere political ends.

This confusion and misunderstanding has not allowed Muslims to take the path of reflecting and meditating on Islam's spiritual values. It has instead created a thick veil that has blinded their eyes to the divine and higher life available in abundance to those who learn and study the book, as expressed in this verse: *'Be Godly by that which you have learned from the book, and by that which you have studied'.* (Al-Imraan: 79)

The Uprooting of Salafi Ideology (Traditional Islamic Thought), Once and for all

As briefly pointed out above, this erroneous concept of an Islamic state has been the cause of war and tragedy, not only in the past but also in the Islamic world today, as demonstrated by the various extremist groups, such as the the Islamic State of Iraq and Syria (ISIS), the Taliban in Afghanistan and the Mullahs of Iran. Not to mention, the Al-Shabaab in Somalia who have destroyed their beautiful land, and the Inqaaz of Sudan who have corrupted and oppressed countless civilians throughout the land.

In addition, consider the Muslim Brotherhood of Egypt, who embarked on a policy of self-empowerment, favouritism, corruption, terrorism and constitutional fraud in less than a year following their rise to power. One does not need to go into the details of the atrocities of the Libyan Muslim Brotherhood and their terrorism, the Al-Qaida of Syria, Iraq and Yemen with their rude and rugged brutality. Let us not forget to mention Hezbollah of Lebanon, Hamas in Palestine, Boko Haram in Nigeria and the rest of the genocides committed on behalf of Islam in many other countries including Mali, Niger, Algeria, Indonesia, Pakistan, etc.

Indeed, this terror of political Islam has spread all over the world and crossed over to Europe and the USA. This evident terror is surely the greatest and most serious threat to the peace and security of the world. It is so serious, that it may put an end to the possibility of human freedom forever.

However, and by the mercy and grace of God, the hypocrisy of the Islamists is beginning to speak for itself, while their influence is beginning to weaken. The corruption of the Islamists' rule in Iran, Egypt, Sudan, Turkey and elsewhere is now evident for all to see. The inclination to dominate in the name of Islam is mostly marred in corruption, totalitarianism, impunity, bad governance and, ultimately, failure, which has now become so loud and clear. This point is further clarified in this book, and also in another book by the same writer titled: 'A New Approach to the Sudanese Crisis'.

Clarifying the great errors of the concept of an Islamic government is the first step to pulling out traditional Islamic thought by the roots, thus paving the way smoothly and easily for the building of a new world based on truth, purity 'Taqwa' and contentment 'Ridwan'. This new world can only be established on the ruins of Salafi and traditional Islamic thought. Consider the verse: *'And those who have founded their house on purity and contentment from Allah'* (Al-Touba: 109).

This book is based on primary insight into correct Islamic thought, true meditation into the Holy Quran and deep contemplation of the deeds of the Great Prophet. Moreover, it is supported by real insight into the actions of the Prophet's great companion Abu Bakr Al-Sideeq[3], and the works of the Prophet's dear brother Ali Ibn Abi Talib[4]. Furthermore, this book is supported by the actions of the noble masters of Islamic Sufism.

There are great expectations of this brief book, such as that it will demolish the foundations of the religious state's house, allowing its roof to fall on top of those who are using this house to deceive others. Achieving this will awaken those who still believe the Islamic state is a valid pursuit, despite all the undeniable suffering it is bringing.

Finally, the writer hopes that the readers will benefit from, and find joy in this important book, which is being published during this critical period in the history of the world.

---

3 *Abu Bakr Al-Sideeq was Prophet Mohammed's close companion, and was the first Caliph after the Prophet's death.*

4 *Ali Ibn Abi Talib was Prophet Mohammed's cousin, student and close companion, also referred to as Imam Ali. He served as Caliph for a brief period, the details of which will be given the next chapter.*

THE FALLACY OF THE ISLAMIC STATE

Chapter
1

28

The Seed of Separation of Islam from the State

The Seed of Separation of Islam from the State in the Actions of Caliph Abu Bakr Al-Sideeq

It is historically established that Muslims were divided into two groups immediately after the death of the Prophet. One group supported Abu Bakr Al-Sideeq, while the other stood by Ali Ibn Abi Talib. It is also known that Ali had reluctantly and after some delay agreed to pledge allegiance to Abu Bakr. Thus, it appeared as if the two groups had been united.

However, ensuing events proved that a great division still persisted. One group insisted on the legitimate right of Ali for succession. The other group seemed to uphold the principle of consultation 'shoora'[5], without defining agreeable criteria, conditions or any clear rules for the selection or appointment of a Caliph. This state of ambiguity led to the Great Upheaval, known as 'Al-Fitna Al-Kubra' in Arabic, in which the companions of the Prophet killed each other in the famous battles of Al-Jamal, Safeen, Naihrawan and other similar painful and cruel tragedies.

---

5 *Shoora is Arabic for 'consultation'. The word is used ambiguously to denote the Islamic method for selecting a Caliph, without a definite method or procedure.*

Looking deeply into this brief two-year period of Abu Bakr's reign, it appears that his period was a mere 'falta' as expressed by his successor Omar Ibn Al-Khattab[6]. The Arabic word 'falta' means 'by chance'. Omar's expression referred to –amongst other things– the fact that Khilaapha, or succession, was not understood as a governance matter, which would have involved planning, management and administrative systems and regulations. It is apparent that Abu Bakr did not even consider himself as the holder of the position of the Head of State. On the day immediately after becoming the Caliph, he planned to continue with his usual business as a merchant, which Omar Ibn Al-Khattab prevented him from doing. One may argue that Abu Bakr planned to continue his business because he was reluctant to earn money by serving as Caliph or Head of State! However, it is not conceivable for a Head of State to find the time and space to be a merchant in order to earn his livelihood. Heads of States by virtue of their office are responsible for governance and management of state affairs such as planning, executive powers, legislation, dealing with foreign kings and diplomatic relations, preparing for wars...etc. Moreover, the engagement of the Head of State in private business amounts to conflict of interest and abuse of power. A ruler must also establish a court from which he will carry out his state responsibilities together with all the management, staffing, workers and equipment. In addition, there are usually security measures for the protection of governors against unforeseen emergencies, since they are responsible for keeping peace and public security.

It seems that the first Caliph was not aware of the scope of his high and critical position as Caliph, and did not understand that

---

6 *Omar Ibn Al-Khattab was a companion of Prophet Mohammed, and served as Caliph for 12 years after Abu Bakr.*

his mission involved the management of an entire state! If the first Caliph was not aware that his job was a full-time paid job, then what kind of state do the political Islam propagandists talk about?

Anyone with modest knowledge of Islamic history will know that during his reign, Abu Bakr had sent Muawiyah Ibn Abi Sufyan[7] to conquer the Levant (present day Syria and Lebanon, 'Alsham' in Arabic) despite the presence of the first Emigrants (the Muhajirun) [8]and the Prophet defenders and protectors (the 'Ansar' or 'helpers'). Muawiyah did not belong to either group because he was one of the released ones[9] , who embraced Islam only at the conquest of Mecca, two years before the death of the Prophet. Abu Bakr's decision to send Muawiyah shows that 'religion' and adherence to Islam were not necessary criteria for choosing political leaders, even during the early days of Islam. During Omar Ibn Al-Khattab's reign, Muawiyah was appointed governor of the entire Levant region. Omar also appointed Amr Ibn Al'as, as governor of Egypt. Amr Ibn Al'as had been one of Islam's fiercest opponents who fought relentlessly against the Prophet. He joined the Muslims together with Muawiyah just before Mecca was conquered. These examples show that

---

7 *Muawiyah was known to have stood against the Prophet in Mecca, and was not a supporter of Islam at all until Mecca was conquered, at which point the Prophet declared him to be 'released', meaning that he was pardoned for his past acts against Islam and was to be set free. Muawiyah later founded the Omayaad Dynasty, which was responsible for establishing the historic illusion of the Islamic state.*

8 *Muhajirun were companions of the Prophet who migrated with him from Mecca to Medina, and included many strong allies of the Prophet, including Abu Bakr, Ali, Omar and a great number of the most devout and strong supporters of Islam.*

9 *'The released ones' refers to the Meccan non-believers, whom the Prophet granted a pardon at the conquest of Mecca, and they embraced Islam as a result of this pardon.*

governance matters, politics and leadership of armies are, and have always been, secular matters, not governed by religious standards. These are the seeds of separation between religion and state in the acts of Abu Bakr.

Furthermore, it is recorded in Islamic history that Abu Bakr, as Caliph, had refused to sit at the Prophet's pulpit in the mosque. In other words, he did not see himself as the Caliph or successor of the Prophet. Thus, the idea that the Prophet is supposed to have a Caliph at all collapsed practically as it collapsed theoretically. In the words of the Quran, the Prophet has greater guardianship on the believers than they have on themselves, so it was not conceivable that one of the believers could replace him and stand in his place. In addition, it is to be noted that Abu Bakr refrained from forcing Ali and Fatima[10] to pledge allegiance to him. This shows that the 'Caliph' did not act as a Head of State with the power to demand and enforce his authority. Indeed, Abu Bakr frankly told Omar to 'take away your Khilaapha and return my religion to me'. You may ponder deeply and reflect on this statement. Abu Bakr referred to religion as 'my' religion, and to Khilaapha as 'your' Khilaapha. Does this not show a clear separation between religion and state?

It is highly probable that Abu Bakr was concerned about the hesitation of the Aus and the Khazraj [11] (the Ansar) towards his

---

10 Fatima was the Prophet's daughter and Ali Ibn Abi Talib (Imam Ali) her husband, who has been previously referred to. His role in the history of Islam is primary and instrumental.

11 The Aus and Khazraj were two of the largest tribes in Medina, who fought each other for a long time before the Prophet helped them to achieve peace. Hence they eventually became fierce supporters of Islam, and are known as 'the Ansar' meaning the defenders

rule, bearing in mind that most of them informed Fatima that they would not have paid allegiance to Abu Bakr had they been aware of her desire that they pledge allegiance to Ali. It is not conceivable that a man of Abu Bakr's status would not have been aware of the virtue of the Ansar, which was revealed in the Quran: *'And those who were the landlords, firmly settled in faith, before them, shower their love to whoever migrates to them'* (Al-Hashr: 9). The Ansar were the original residents of Medina, who protected, supported and brought victory to the Prophet. In fact, the Ansar were the triumphant battalion of Islam, 'gathering in multitude in times of need, and retreating back in times of greed' as expressed by the Prophet, praising the Ansar. Abu Bakr must have recalled the many occasions where the Prophet praised the Ansar, especially this Hadith[12]: 'If all people walked on a valley, and the Ansar took another, I would walk with the Ansar'; or this Hadith: 'If it was not for the Hijra[13], I would have loved to be one of the Ansar'.

Also, it is established that Sa'd Ibn Ubaada, one of Medina's leaders who embraced Islam quite early, refused to pledge allegiance to Abu Bakr. The Prophet is reported to have said about Sa'd: 'May Allah's prayers and mercy be bestowed upon the family of Sa'd Ibn Ubaada'. There is no doubt that the refusal of Sa'd, who was the chief of the Khazraj tribe, to support Abu Bakr caused the latter to feel that the office of Khilaapha was forced on him, since it lacked the support of many whose credibility was beyond doubt. Did Abu Bakr not say 'I am awarded authority over

---

and helpers for victory.

12 Hadith is the Arabic terminology for the sayings and statements of the Prophet.

13 Hijra is Arabic for 'migration'. Here the Prophet is pointing to his migration from Mecca to Medina.

you, and I am not the best of you'? In other words, he did not ask to be Caliph, rather it was imposed on him.

It was not only most of the Aus and Khazraj who refrained from supporting Abu Bakr, but also Bani Hashim [14], who were not even present at Saqifa Bani Saida[15] where allegiance to Abu Bakr was sworn. In addition, many of the closest companions to the Prophet supported Ali Ibn Abi Talib rather than Abu Bakr, including: Abu Thar Al- Ghifari, Ammar Ibn Yasir, Al-Muqdad Ibn Amr, Osama Ibn Zaid and many others. It is certain that Abu Bakr was well aware of the virtues and status of these great men. It is highly unlikely that Abu Bakr was not aware of the Prophet's Hadith praising Abu Thar Al-Ghifari: 'Neither the sky nor the earth accommodated one more truthful than Abu Thar, save for the Prophets'. The Prophet also one day said 'Woe unto Abu Thar, he lives alone, dies alone, and is resurrected alone'. This Hadith points to the seeds of individualism, independence, acuity and resolve, acquired by this great companion of the Prophet.

The books of history also tell us that Fatima, the daughter of the Prophet, did not accept Abu Bakr as Caliph, and she refused to pledge allegiance to him throughout her life. Abu Bakr made several attempts to win her support, but they were in vain. It is also established that Abu Bakr fiercely opposed Omar's suggestion to burn alive both Fatima and Ali for their continued refusal to recognise Abu Bakr's authority. This incident alone is sufficient to truly expose the fallacy contained within the concept of an Islamic state. If the establishment of a religious state was

---

14 Bani Hashim is the name of the family line of the Prophet.

15 This is the famous name of the place where allegiance was pledged to Abu Bakr to be Caliph following the departure of the Prophet.

one of Islam's religious requirements, or one of its founding or primary pillars, the Prophet himself would have named his successor. Fatima and Abu Bakr in particular could not have been in any dispute over it, with both of them being so highly esteemed in Islam without any shred of a doubt. Every Muslim knows that Fatima was the most honoured in the Prophet's house, as revealed in the Holy Quran: *'Allah only desires to remove impurity away from you Oh family of the House, and to purify you again and again'* (Al-Ahzaab: 33). On the other hand, Abu Bakr was also one of the Prophet's closest companions and is referred to as the 'second of two', being the Prophet's principal companion during the Hijra. This was expressed in the Quran: *'Second of two, as they are both in the cave, and he says to his companion: Do not be sorrowful, Allah is with us'* (Al-Touba: 40).

Do you want the truth? The Islamic state is a calamity, and Khilaapha is a trap. It is a calamity and a trap that led to the massive slaughter of the Prophet's companions, created animosity and spread hatred amongst Muslims. It is the work of the mind's Satan, as the Quran points out: *'Satan only desires to inflict animosity and hatred amongst you'* (Al-Mai'da: 91)

As pointed out earlier, Abu Bakr himself made a clear separation between religion and state, and articulated this in his timeless statement: 'Take away your Khilaapha, and return my religion to me'. This is exactly what Abu Bakr did in practice, when he handed over the Khilaapha back to Omar and appointed him in his place without referring to a Shoora (consultation) or considering the views of others. This turn of events is satisfactory proof that Abu Bakr did not regard Khilaapha to be a state affair, or a religious duty.

The Seed of Separation of Islam from State in the Actions of Imam Ali Ibn Abi Talib

It is established in history that Ali Ibn Abi Talib firmly believed that he was the first Caliph after the Prophet Mohammed. This belief is understandable considering that Ali was the first young man to embrace Islam since childhood, being raised by the Prophet himself. Ali was also famous for his well-recognised knowledge of the deep secret meanings of the Quran. Ali has been a close ally of the Prophet in the realm of spirituality. For example the Prophet once said: 'I am the City of Knowledge, and Ali is the door to it'. He also stated: 'Ali to me is of the same station as Aaron is to Moses', and: 'I am close to whoever is close to Ali'.

The Prophet entrusted Ali with the affairs of Medina during the Battle of Tabouk, and allowed him to sleep on the Prophet's own bed during the night of the Hijra. The Prophet continuously entrusted Ali with his own family affairs. Ali was married to the Prophet's daughter and was father to his beloved grandchildren. In addition, Ali was a leading Quran script-writer and coordinator of the Prophet's important correspondence and covenants. He always supported the Prophet as Aaron had always corroborated Moses. The Prophet raised Ali to the status of equality to himself when it came to earnest prayer or meditation ('Al-Mubahala'[16]). Al-Mubahala was stated in the Quran as follows: *'And whosoever argues with you about this, after that knowledge which was revealed to you, say to them: Come. Let's gather our sons and your sons, our women and your women, ourselves and yourselves, and let us pray earnestly, and then invoke the curse of Allah upon the liars'* (Al-Imraan: 61). In Mubahala, sharp and clear knowledge puts an end to any argument, as expressed in the

---

16 *Mubahala is Arabic for earnest prayer or meditation.*

Quran. It is well known and an established historical fact that the Prophet interpreted the verse of Almubahala in the following way: 'Our sons' to mean Al-Hassan and Al-Husain, his grandsons from Fatima and Ali; 'Our women' to mean Fatima, and 'Ourselves" to mean Ali.

The Prophet further confirmed the equality of himself with Ali in the episode of 'brotherhood' between the Muhajirun[17] and the Ansar,[18] where the Prophet initiated a brotherhood bond with Ali, who was a Muhaajir like the Prophet. In the 'brotherhood' episode, Mohammed initiated brotherhood bonds between the emigrants from Mecca on the one hand and the Ansar or 'helpers' in Medina on the other. It was not initiated amongst the 'emigrants'. This is how Muslim sages knew that Ali was the Prophet's brother in the realm of spirituality and essence, and his cousin and son-in-law in the domain of form.

In confirmation of this precious meaning, the Prophet clearly distinguished between his 'companions' and his 'brothers' in his famous Hadith: 'Oh, how much I long for my brothers who have not yet come!'. Asked three times by his companions: 'Are we not your brothers oh Messenger of Allah?' He replied: 'You are my companions'. So one of the companions asked: 'Who are your brothers oh Messenger of Allah?' He replied: 'A people who will come at the ending of time, the work of one of them is rewarded as much as the work of seventy of you'. This meaning has been reiterated numerous times by the Prophet. See for example this

---

17 Muhajirun is Arabic for emigrants. Here the reference is to those who migrated from Mecca to Medina, whom the Prophet had equated in brotherhood with the Ansar.

18 The Ansar is Arabic for defenders or helpers. Here the reference is to the Medina residents who stood by the Prophet and defended him.

Hadith: 'The best of the believers are those who believed in me without ever seeing me'. Or this Hadith: 'People from my nation, who are neither prophets, nor martyrs, and their abode is aspired to, by prophets and martyrs'. In this Hadith of the Prophet there is a subtle reference to the 'brothers' of the Prophet. The Hadith refers to the ending of the concept of the Prophet as mediator between man and God (Khatm Al-Nubuwa). Also, this Hadith refers to the ending of the concept of martyrdom through Jihad/Holy War.

Therefore, Ali was in fact one of the Prophet's 'brothers', though he was considered one of the companions. This is the point Ali was making when he stated 'If the veil is lifted, I will not be more certain'. This is the reason that explains why Ali was not instructed by the Prophet to meet Uwais Al-Qurani[19], but rather instructed Abu Bakr and Omar and required them to ask Uwais to pray for both of them. When Abu Bakr and Omar met Uwais, he asked them: 'Are you the two companions of Mohamed? And have you seen him?' When they answered 'Yes', he responded with this timeless statement: 'By the name of Allah, you have not seen him, except as one would claim to see a sword inside its sheath'. Had Ali been present, Uwais could not have made such a statement. Ali is therefore one of the Prophet's brothers, but the order of the day at that time fell short of his ascent to the abodes of individualism.

I would not wish to leave this point without referring to an exquisite dialogue between Ali in his last days, and his son

---

19 *Uwais Al-Qurani was born and lived in Yemen. He embraced Islam without ever meeting the Prophet. It has been reported that the Prophet instructed some of his companions to ask him to pray if they ever met him. Uwais outlived the Prophet, and the companions Abu Bakr and Omar did meet him and asked for his prayer according to the Prophet's instructions.*

Mohamed Ibn Al-Hanafiya. Mohamed asked his father: 'Who is greater, you or Abu Bakr?' Ali replied: 'Abu Bakr is greater'. Mohamed asked again mentioning Omar. Ali again confirmed that Omar is greater than him. Mohamed then said: 'So I decided to keep silent. Lest I asked about Osman, and he would have replied: "Osman is greater too". So instead I asked him: "Father, who you are?" Ali replied: "I am one of the Muslims".

With this eloquent and wise response, Imam Ali ascended high above Khilaapha and the false concept of a religious state, reaching to the abode of the Muslims who are the 'brothers' of the Prophet, who have been subtly referred to in the Quran: *'Who speaks more perfect than one who calls for God, performs good deeds and declares that he is one of the Muslims?'* (Fussilat: 33). Calling for God is a high spiritual call, and not a mere ritual task, as currently practiced by ignorant Islamists. It is one of the noble qualities of those who possess an excellent command of the book, "Ilm Al-Kitaab", which is the 'total and complete knowledge of the book'. Such knowers of the book must also have witnessed what God himself witnesses, as expressed clearly by the Quran addressing Mohamed: *'Say: Allah's witnessing is adequately sufficient witnessing between you and me. In the same way, the one who possesses Ilm Al-Kitaab is such an adequate witness'* (Al-Ra'ad: 43). This high spiritual call for God is a call for peace. Only Allah is capable of such call, or one guided by Allah onto the straight path: *'Allah calls for the abode of peace, and guides unto the straight path, those who will'* (Yunus: 25).

It is needless to emphasise the fact that, amongst the companions, Ali was the most knowledgeable about the Quran. The Caliph Omar Ibn Al-Khattab used to say whenever he is challenged by a puzzling religious question: 'This case is only for Aba Alhassan (Ali) to resolve'. Moreover, the Prophet once stated: 'The Quran turns with Ali, therefore turn with Ali wherever he turns'. In fact this Hadith alone is sufficient to prove the high status of Ali. Ali was also a well-recognised leader amongst the companions in defending and protecting the Prophet in the battlefield. Furthermore, Fatima's decisive and firm stance regarding Ali's right to succession of the Prophet was a major factor in Ali's insistence, determination and refusal to pledge allegiance to Abu Bakr. Ali only accepted to swear allegiance to Abu Bakr after Fatima's death.

However, I believe, and in fact assert, that the fallacy of the Islamic state was directly revealed to Ali. Therefore, he completely relinquished the idea of succession in his later life. There is incalculable evidence in support of this assertion. For instance:

1. Coming back from the Nahrwan battle, [20] Ali's heart was heavy with grief because he had killed four thousand or more of his own companions and the companions of the Prophet. The Iraqi river Tigris was immersed in blood. After this battle, Imam Ali used to say repeatedly: 'When will its "most wretched" appear?' He was referring to the Prophet's statement when he asked Ali: 'Alas Ali, do you know who "its most wretched" is?' Ali responded: 'The one who hamstrung the she-camel of Salih?'. The Prophet replied: 'No, Ali. Its most wretched is the one who

---

20 *Nahrawan battle took place in 659 AD, between Ali and his followers who departed from him 'The Khawaarij' after the Battle of Safeen.*

cleaves this (putting his hand on Ali's forehead), and colours this in blood (putting his hand on Ali's beard)'. Thus, Ali was yearning for his own death, having realised that the bloodshed was a trap. He felt that his mission was now complete, and that it was time to accomplish important work. There is no doubt that Ali would have been reviewing this long journey of wars that he had to go through against the Prophet's companions for the purposes of an Islamic state that have in the end yielded nothing but blood and misery. Let us listen to Ali in those remote days, as he used to tap his chest saying: 'There is vast knowledge here, if only I could find ones to carry it'. We will see that Ali has found in his son Al-Hassan the capacity to carry some of that knowledge.

2. In the Battle of Safeen[21], Muawiyah's army was composed of 100,000 men, while Ali had 80,000. Ali's army was able to almost defeat Muawiyah's, but Amr Ibn Al'as, who was leading Muawiyah's army, decided to raise the Holy Quran on top of the lances signifying the desire for arbitration. Realising that this was a mere trick, Ali announced it to be 'A word of truth intended for falsehood'. However, Ali's companions forced him to accept arbitration, the result of which was yet another trick by which Ali was deprived of Khilaapha by his companion Abu Musa Al-Asha'ri! Ali refused to accept this result, and addressed his companions in the famous Arabic saying: 'I gave you my advice at the bend during the night, but you failed to realise the clarity of its truth until the forenoon of the next day'. Ali used to frequently say to his companions: 'My views were corrupted by your ill-advice'.

3. In the Battle of Al-Jamal [22], Ali found himself in a position where he was fighting Aisha, the 'mother of the believers'

---

21 *The famous Battle of Safeen took place in 658 AD.*

22 *Al-Jamal battle took place in 656 AD.*

and wife of the Prophet, in addition to her allies Talha and Al-Zubeir[23], and some of the best companions of the Prophet. The situation being so grim, it was quite understandable and almost inevitable for Ali to reconsider the basis for this whole matter of the Islamic State. For what purpose is this blood of the companions being spilled? Ali was of course well aware of the Prophet's instruction to his companions in the last year before he departed: 'Do not become disbelievers after me, and start beheading each other'.

4. From the very beginning, Ali found himself in the difficult and embarrassing situation, where he was compelled to fight with Abu Bakr on this question of the Islamic State. Both Ali and Abu Bakr were fully aware of the virtue of each other. Abu Bakr was the Prophet's companion, who was praised by the Prophet, who said: 'Abu Bakr is not the best of you because of his prayer or fasting, but because of a deep secret in his heart'. Certain verses of the Holy Quran spoke highly of both men. Abu Bakr was described in the Quran as the 'second of two', and Ali, as the 'peaceful one' with the Prophet in the verse: *'Allah sets forth a parable of a man with divided partners quarrelling inside him, and another man who is peaceful with another'* (Al-Zumur: 29). The Prophet commented: 'Ali is peaceful with me'. Also, when the Quran was revealed: *'So that an attentive ear may be conscious of it'* (Al-Haqqah: 12), the Prophet said: 'That is Ali's ear'. All of these sayings must have been vivid in the minds of these two great men during those days.

5. Imam Ali must have noticed that the Islamic state for him was like a mirage. Whenever it came close, and he thought he caught it, it slipped away from his fingers. Even when he did

---

23 *Two of the most well-known of the Prophet's companions.*

become Caliph following the death of Othman[24], he spent the four years of his reign in continuous wars. In other words, Ali had not in fact assumed the role of Caliph at any time. This was a clear sign to Ali that it had not been Allah's will that he was to become a Caliph. This fact was indeed understood by Ali in his last days, and also by those Muslim knowers of truth after Ali, who stated that 'We have known Allah through the undoing of our will'. When a Muslim, who is a knower of truth decides on a matter, having planed it perfectly, and sees that it is still not accomplished, he will instantly understand that Allah willed it not. This is why Ali did not return to Medina, the seat of Khilaapha after the Battle of Nahrawan. Instead he decided to stay in Kufa, still repeating: 'When will its most wretched appear?' Allah answered his cry, and 'its most wretched' turned out to be one of his own companions.

Ali used to say: 'I am more familiar with the ways of the heavens than with those of the earth'. His friend and companion Ammar Ibn Yasir, the beloved of the Prophet, was defending Ali during the Battle of Safeen, saying: 'Mohammed fought against you over the bringing down of the Quran (Tanzeel). Today, we fight against you over its original meaning (Taweel)', until Ammar himself was killed at the hands of the transgressing group, while he was reiterating the word of Taweel. The word of Taweel was the password and the secret code that Ali understood.

Accordingly, Ali turned away from the fallacious concept of an Islamic state, and turned his face towards the heavens, where the true kingdom is to be found. He then veered towards his city, the spiritual city of hearts, about which the Prophet said: 'I am the city of knowledge, and Ali is the door to it'. Thus, Ali kept close to Allah, and his heart opened up with the Taweel of the Book, where the truth is hidden. Ali was referring to this truth

---

24 Othman Ibn Affan served as third Caliph after Abu Bakr and Omar.

when he used to tap his chest and say: 'Here is vast knowledge, if only I could find ones to carry it'. So did Ali find those carriers? We will soon find out.

6. After Ali's forehead was cleaved by Abdel Rahman Ibn Muljam[25], he remained conscious for three days before passing away. His companions requested him to appoint his son Al-Hassan as successor but Ali declined their request, saying: 'I will neither instruct you, nor forbid you'. This answer indicates that Ali has now become quite neutral about the matter of succession and Khilaapha. If the Khilaapha was a religious matter, then Al-Hassan would have been the perfect and ideal successor being the most favoured in the nation and a master amongst the youth of heaven. The Prophet said about Al-Hassan 'This son of mine is a master, and Allah will use him to resolve conflict and create peace between two fighting groups of Muslims'.

On the basis of the above-mentioned, I would certainly assert that Ali was the one who inspired his son Al-Hassan to make peace with Muawiyah. It was virtually impossible for Al-Hassan to extend his hand to a man who was the enemy not just of his father, but also of his grandfather and had been an enemy of the whole clan of Bani Hashim[26]. Al-Hassan would not have sworn allegiance to Muawiyah without clear instruction from his father, Ali, and a latent sign from his grandfather, the Prophet. Al-Hassan himself proved this assertion, when, at the outset of his speech, he relinquished power to Muawiyah, declaring: 'Allah guided you through our first one (referring to Prophet Mohammad), and spared your blood through our last (referring to himself)'. With this timeless expression, Al-Hassan was able to bring the religion back to its pure source, where guidance spares blood

---

25 The name of Ali's companion who killed Ali.

26 Bani Hashim is the house in the tribe of Quraish to which the Prophet and his family belonged.

and peace is allowed to spread its wings. Where the balance of true virtue is brought down on the earth, and where Allah's blessing upon the inhabitants of the earth is fulfilled.

However, events did not go in the direction intended by Al-Hassan, this honorable and graceful leader. Soon afterwards he was betrayed by Muawiyah. He was poisoned and died in unclear circumstances where fingers pointed to Muawiyah. It is certain that Al-Hassan had accepted his inevitable destiny. Was he not the one who said: 'One who trusts in whatever Allah elects, would not desire any state other than "what is". May peace be upon Al-Hassan amongst all creation.

This malicious betrayal by Muawiyah caused Al-Hussein to depart from the correct path of his brother Al-Hassan. He refused to pledge allegiance to Yazid, son of Muawiyah, who assumed the throne of the Islamic state after his father. Al-Hussein decided to resort to Kufa, until he was killed in the famous Battle of Karbala on 10th Muharram in the 61st year of Hijra, the Day of Ashoora. On that day the army of Yazid Ibn Muawiyah killed Al-Hussein together with seventy members of the Prophet's family, thereby covering the Islamic world in a wave of gloomy darkness.

During those dark years, the Omayyad army was able to stamp out the good forefathers of the Prophet's companions, who were massacred and exterminated, including members of the Awus and Khazraj tribes in the Battle of Dhat Al-Harra. In this battle, the Prophet's indomitable stronghold Medina was desecrated. Then, the same atrocious hands extended to Mecca where the Ka'ba itself was attacked by catapults, and fear was spread in the House of God where Abdulla Ibn Al-Zubeir and others were killed. The false idea of the Islamic state was then victorious, and had turned into an oppressive rule, handed from father to son. Mischief can only breed misery and disaster.

THE FALLACY OF THE ISLAMIC STATE

Chapter 2

True Islam is based on Separation of Religion from the State

The land of Islam rose again from the ashes, despite the killing of the best companions of the Prophet. The grace of Allah preserved the Book. The Holy Quran states: *'We knew that they never decrease, even beneath the earth, as the book is forever preserved'* (Quaaf: 4). It is due to Allah's kindness to man and His preservation of His religion that Master Ali Zein Al-Abideen,- one of Al-Hussein's intelligent sons - was saved from death in the Karbilaa' massacre. Ali Zein Alabideen was able to bring Islam back to its pure source, manifesting the message of peace and reconciliation of his uncle Al-Hassan. This was the seed of Islamic Sufism, which was built upon correct and sound understanding of the core message of Islam laid out in the Quran and the Sunnah.

It is interesting to notice that in its subtle meaning, the word Karbilaa' in ancient Babylonian language means 'closeness or proximity to Allah'. Also, linguists tell us that in the Assyrian language Karbilaa' is composed of two words: 'Karb' meaning 'sacred place', and 'il' meaning Allah. The complete meaning of the word in Assyrian becomes: 'The sacred place of Allah'. In Arabic however, the word indicates woe, anguish and affliction. It seems that the inward meaning of the word is referring to Al-Hussein's and his companions' proximity to Allah, as they live in His safe and sacred domain, while the outward meaning refers to anguish and affliction for those who committed their murder in that battle.

It is to be noted that great Sufi teachers who had founded the City of Knowledge through purity and clarity, had never recognised any form of Islamic state.

Master Ali Zein Al-Abideen abandoned the Khilaapha and distanced his good self from the erroneous idea of an Islamic state altogether. Instead, he gave all his attention single-mindedly to devotion and worship. He was known as 'Al-Sajjaad', meaning 'one who is plentiful, abundant and continuous in prostration'. Such noble qualities opened the doors of 'Wilaaya'[27] for master Ali Zein Alabideen. The Quran puts it thus: *'Your guardians are only Allah and his Messenger and the faithful believers, who pray and offer zakat while they prostrate'* (Al-Mai'da: 55). It is established in Islamic history that this verse was revealed in praise of Ali Ibn Abi Talib. Ali Zein Al-Abideen has taken this same path and followed the footprints of his grandfather Ali Ibn Abi Talib, thereby paving the way for Islamic Sufisim (Tasawuf). Tasawuf is based on a total separation between religion and the state.

In this connection, it is worthwhile narrating a wonderful story. History informs us that one day, Hisham Ibn Abd-Elmalik, the then Crown Prince of the Omayyad Dynasty, was in Mecca on pilgrimage. He was trying to approach the scared 'black stone' to kiss it - as part of the usual Islamic ritual in pilgrimage - but was unable to as the jammed crowds stood in his way. His entourage set up a throne for him facing the Ka'ba to preserve his prestige. However, Hisham and his companions were taken by surprise, as

---

27 *Wilaaya is Arabic for proximity. The word is used in the Quran. Sufis use it to indicate a station that is preserved for those closest to Allah and are free from fear and sorrow. The singular is' Wali', and plural 'Awliyaa'.*

a man with so much dignity and solemnity approached the black stone. The crowds around the Ka'ba started to give way in respect and reverence, and allowed the man the space to be the only circumambulator around the Ka'ba. Amazed at this fantastic scene, Hisham exclaimed about this strange man, pretending not to recognize Ali Zein Al-Abidcen. At this point the famous Arab poet, Al Farazdaq, who was present with the Crown Prince, instantly delivered his famous poem in response to Hisham's enquiry about Ali Zein Al-Abideen. The famous poet said:

This is the one,

Whose weight and trod of feet,

are recognised by this land,

And even the Holy House knows who is who,

This is the son of the best of all,

This is the pure,

The immaculate,

The Chaste, and the Master,

Your denial does not harm or belittle his status,

Since he is recognised by Arabs,

As well as none-Arabs.

This is how the early light of the spiritual kingdom of Islamic Sufism began to shine, through purity, immaculateness, chastity and knowledge, spreading the light of the Sufi teachers amongst Arabs and non-Arabs. The values of Islam shifted from a narrow political state to the core of the religion itself, as confirmed by Al-Farazdaq again:

Allah bestowed upon him honour and status,

From the beginning of time,

Thus his destiny was written.

Furthermore, Al-Farazdaq aimed to assure the Crown Prince that Sufi masters such as Ali Zein Al-Abideen will never stoop to deception or betrayal. They are not greedy for status in an Islamic state, which they had renounced. They are generous and honorable people with great virtue, as the Quran describes the Prophet: *'You are virtuous with great morals'* (Al-Qualam: 4). Al-Farazdaq continued in praise of Ali Zein Al-Abideen, saying:

So affably easy, you cannot fear his approaches.

He is groomed in virtue and steeped in generosity.

It is notable that Al-Farazdaq did not give eulogy to Zein Al-Abideen in terms of power or authority, but he praised him as a master in purity, good deeds, love and perfection:

If you mention those who have purity, they are the masters.

And if you enquire about the best people on earth,

They will be the answers.

Their love fends evil and wickedness away,

Showering perfection and goodness, and showing the way.

This is how, in the midst of a gloomy night, the stars of Sufi teachers began to shine, and a tree of chastity and devotion and austerity began to grow, unfold and flourish. During the first Hijri century, great masters started to appear, such as master Al-Hassan Al-Basri. More masters appeared during the second and third centuries, including: Ibrahim Ibn Adham, Al-Surri Al-Saqti, Abu Yazid Al-Bastami, Ma'aroof Al-Karkhi, Al-Shibli culminating with the glittering star of Abu Al-Gasim Al-Jinaid. Followed by the famous Al-Hallaj, who was martyred at the beginning of the fourth Hijri century, in one of the greatest epics of redemption, bravery and challenge against totalitarianism and the false religious state, which denies freedom of thought. Besides Al-Hallaj, many have been victims to the oppressive Islamic state rule, such as Al-Sahrwardi, who was killed by one of the Islamic governments in the sixth Hijri century.

Despite these challenges and obstacles, the victorious march of Islamic Sufism continued. People who were desirous and thirsty for truth and for God, departed from political authority and state affairs, and turned to Sufi masters. In the sixth Hijri century, Al-Ghazali wrote his famous book 'Revival of Religious Knowledge'. It is a book, which is closer to traditional doctrine but had more equability and depth than the prevailing knowledge of the time. This paved the way for subsequent masters whose knowledge flourished and yielded ripe fruits, lifting Sufisim to a great pinnacle, with the appearance of the great masters Jailaani and Badawi, followed by Master Disooqi and Master Rufa'i in the sixth century.

The seventh Hijri century flowed with masters and Sufi teachers such as Abu Al-Hassan Al-Shazali, all the way to the advent of the greatest master Muhieddin Ibn Arabi. Ibn Arabi is one of the best 'knowers of truth', famous for his book: 'Al-Futuhat Al-Makkiyya' (The Meccan's Illuminations) and 'Fusoos Al-Hikam' (Bezels of Wisdom), and hundreds of other letters on divine love, oneness of existence and many more wonderful and exquisite writings.

Many more masters continued to emerge, illuminating the long dim night, which enveloped the Muslim world. We cannot, and need not mention all of these masters and their writings. This can be investigated elsewhere by checking relevant sources. However, I would like for readers to stop a little at master Abdul-Ghani Al-Nabulsi who lived in the eleventh and twelfth Hijri centuries. He was a great creative master, and a wonderful poet. His most famous work is his poetry collection 'The Divan of Truths and Collection of Delicacies', and 'The Wine of the Tavern, and the Ring of Melodies.

In concluding the reference to the spiritual kingdom of Sufism and true knowledge, we must mention the grand master Ustadh Mahmoud Mohammed Taha, who lived in the fourteenth Hijri century and the beginning of the fifteenth (1912-1985) in Sudan. He is the perfect, wondrous and eerie master, and the founder of what he termed 'Second Message of Islam'. This great sage was assassinated by one of the false and pseudo Islamic governments, after trying him on a charge of apostasy.

It goes without saying that all of the great masters mentioned above have completely renounced the Islamic state, and moved away from its trap. In return, Allah showered them with a rich life of peace, stability and love.

Let us now point briefly to the 'State' as envisioned in Islamic Sufism.

The Vision of the State in Islamic Sufi Thought

The great Sufi teachers realised with total certitude, through experience, revelation and direct perception, that the human being is the world. For this reason, they were not deceived and distracted by the struggle for power. They did not occupy their time with this false idea of an Islamic state. Listen to Ibn Arabi as he declares:

And you claim to be a small entity,

but in you the greatest world is embodied.

Thus, a correct religious insight confirms that God is the hidden treasure concealed under the wall of mind and thought as is clear from this piece of poetry by Al-Nabulsi:

You are the treasure behind all this,

And the enigma is the mind and thoughts

As a master realises the treasure inside himself, he receives spiritual ecstasy and eternal joy. This is the glorified 'State' of Islam, which is present in every moment. Let us hear Al-Nabulsi singing again:

This is our 'State', it is now present.

The State of glory, and the treasure of joy.

About this ecstasy, Master Ibrahim Ibn Adham says: 'We live in such ecstasy, that if it is known by kings, they would fight us over it with swords'. The same meaning was expressed by master Ibn Al-Faarid,

There is with me an ecstasy, before I was born,

It is with me always, even after the decay of my bone.

When Ibn Arabi says:

'We have a state that appears at the ending of time.

It appears unhidden like the sunshine'

Ibn Arabi is referring here to that timeless ecstasy, and the word 'state', is only a terminology. In the same way the term Kingdom of Heaven was used to describe this state of mind, but the ignorant could not sense and understand that hidden meaning. Al-Nabulsi says:

Burn the ignorant in his crude form of his ideology,

Since he does not sense the meaning of the terminology.

The expression 'at the ending of time' refers to the ending of the concept of time in our mind, by seeing the essence of truth contained inside the shells of time. This is how masters understand the 'state' of Ibn Arabi. Hear Al-Nabulsi again saying:

It is true that universes are being folded and unfolded,

And in the shells of times, therein is the jewel of truth

As told by Muhi Eldin [28] who is the grand authority,

We have a state that appears at the ending of time,

And it appears unhidden like the sunhine

It is the state of the human body, referred to as the 'shadow' in the statement of Master Alrufaa'i as he addresses the essence of Prophet Mohammed in himself:

This is the state of shadows.

It has arrived

So extend your right hand, for my lips to behold.

---

28 Nabulsi is referring here to Muhiddin Ibn Arabi

The suffering Sufi Al-Tigani Yousif Bashir[29] painted a beautiful inner picture of the 'State' of Sufism in his wonderful poem:

A state made of light parades

Surrounding a blooming world of poetry brides

Its crown is woven with the aspiration of the full moon,

And its banner is raised with grandeur

We have given it authority,

Where the king instructs not,

And the Emir (prince) orders not.

A new book about Al-Tigani is under preparation, titled: 'Al-Tigani: A String of the sanctified flute, and the remainder of holy messengers'

---

29 *Bashir is a Sudanese poet who lived at the beginning of the 20th century. The Suffering Sufi is the title of one of his poems.*

THE FALLACY OF THE ISLAMIC STATE

Chapter 3

The Islamic State A Fallacy with no Foundation in the Holy Quran

(Avoid seeing the whole as apart. It is an ordeal, the ramification of which is not restricted to the unfair alone. Beware! Allah's punishment is severe) «Alanfal: 35»

To find out whether the concept of the Islamic state is supported by the Quran, it is necessary and of high importance to undertake a thorough review and a careful study of the verses of the Quran. What does the Quran claim to be? What is the Quran all about?

The Holy Quran is looked upon by all Muslims as the embodiment of the eternal truth, and the word of Allah (the Islamic absolute and supreme God of all the worlds). It was revealed at the heights of heavens and gushily flowed from the lips of the Prophet of Islam easily and fluently in Arabic words in the Quranic Surahs, and in images of shortened intermittent Alphabets as the opening verses of some Quranic Surahs. The words and the letters of the Quran are refined phrases and sublime linguistic structures beautified with subtle significations. It is euphonic and relaxing. The Quran is described metaphorically as a tree; at the top, fruits are superabundant and at the bottom, the deep roots are sparkling in plentiful waters.

The Quran originated from the zenith of the timeless, and poured filling the valleys of eternity. The Quran states: *'Bestow upon him refuge till he hears the words of Allah'* (Al-Touba: 6).

The words of Allah are one of His attributes, which were always here! Which are here now! And which will always be here, endless and beginning-less.

The words of the Quran are not just words. They are the essence of creation as confirmed in the Quran: *'If only a Quran whereby the mountains were set in motion, or the earth were cleft, or the dead were spoken to'* (Al-Ra'ad: 31). The Quran, when properly understood, is a book of supreme high status, protected from falsehood. It is a book springing from the abode of the exalted summits *'Falsehood cannot touch this book, from front or from behind, it is descending from the abode of the All-wise, All-praiseworthy'* (Fussilat: 42). The Quran is pure spirit: *'Thus we have revealed to you the spirit of our order (highest order)'* (Shoora: 52). The divine illumination and the intelligible plain wisdom of the Quran are evident manifestations of Allah the Exalted. The rays of the lights of Quran do not shine over Muslims only, but they are gleaming over all mankind *'O, mankind, there have come to you a conclusive final proof from your Lord, and We have sent down to you a clear light'* (Al-Nisa': 174).

The Quran in its majestic splendor and grandeur is free from all doubts. The Quran only guides those who are pure and taintless: *'Alif-Lam-Meem, * This is the Book that doubt cannot touch, it is a guidance for the pure and the taintless'* (Al-Baqara: 1&2). Alif Laam, Meem are Arabic letters, not words. Some Surahs begin with shortened intermittent letters. This verse in the Surah Al-Bagara is an example. Another example is the first verse in Surah Al-Zukhruf, which reads as follows *'Ha- Meem * These are the verses of the comprehensible book of illumination * We have made the Book, an Arabic Quran in order that you might understand * And indeed it is, in the Mother of the Book at our* *supreme abode, is exalted and intelligible'* (Al-Zukhruf: 1, 2, 3, 4). These verses indicate clearly that the Quran is exalted and subtle and above all languages. It is beyond words. Ha, Meem are two Arabic letters corresponding to H, and M respectively. Accordingly, the meaning of the verse will be: The shortened intermittent alphabets (Ha, Meem), in the mother of the book (the source of the book), are high and more decisive than the limitations of language. However, the Quran was revealed in Arabic in order to be understood by the first people the Quran addressed - i.e. Arabic speaking people.

As indicated above, the words of the Quran are pure spirit. How can the spirit be deformed, shaped and limited into a constitution or law? How can the spirit be watered down, adjusted and reorganised by legislative councils?

If falsehood cannot touch the Quran from the front (the future) or from behind (the past), how can it be promulgated as a law like any other law, which is subject to amendment, renewal and cancellation!

How can Allah (the Exalted), whose light fills space, time and flows over to the endless shores of the timeless, be subject to legislative procedures, which are restricted by the limited consciousness of the legislators?

If the Quran is the ultimate proof and the light of God, how can the light of God be a constitution or a piece of legislation?

Do Islamist propagators –whom we know very well– understand the proof of God? Did they see His light? Is there any person who is competent to materialise the light of the sun into a law, let alone the perfect light of God!

If the Quran is free from doubts, it cannot be reduced and minimised into a changing legislation.

To allege that the Quran is a constitution is very naïve, immature and superficial. Such an allegation is invalid and amounts to a mere lie used to exploit the masses under the blessed name of Allah. The Quran is greater than all of the political propaganda of the Islamists. It is stated in the Quran that we cannot touch its deep meanings, luminous knowledge and perpetuity, unless Allah purifies our heart again and again: *'Indeed, it is a noble Quran * Hidden in a preserved concealed Book * None can touch except after being purified * It is a revelation from the Lord of the worlds'* (Al-Waquia'a: 77, 78, 79, 80). This Purification is referred to in another book by the writer titled: (Imageries on the Margins of the Hearts and the Advent of the Intellectual Revolution).

The Quran states in a wonderful parallelism: *'If this Quran had been sent down to address a mountain, you would surely have seen the mountain humbling itself submissively, being shuttered, and rendered asunder out of the apprehension of Allah'* (Al-Hashr: 21). It is impossible to reduce such timeless attributes of the Quran to a mere constitution, statute or regulation. The words of God are as absolute as God and shall continue to be so up to the fading away of everything into nothingness.

On the other hand, a constitution is human aspiration and hope for higher values, laid down in legal terminologies and jargons, which are all blemished by the brain's barriers and imperfections. Statutes are more limited than the constitution. The Quran is the word of God where all evolution rests and comes to an end at His supreme abode: *'And that to your Lord is the finality'* (Alnajm: 42) i.e. the finality of finality!

The Quran speaks metaphorically about the supernatural and the unseen beyond the beyond: *'And they veil that, which is beyond, which is the truth'* (Al-Baqara: 91). Can any legislator, however competent and of outstanding abilities, drag the unseen, the supernatural, the paranormal and the prophets' miracles and combine all that grandeur into limited constitutions and petty statutes? Certainly, the answer should be no.

The crucial question is: What do the advocates of the so-called Islamic state want to apply from the verses of the Quran? Do they want to apply all, or some, of the Quranic verses? There are six thousand two hundred and thirty six (6236) verses (Ayat) in the Quran.

Now, let us classify and analyse the topics mentioned in the Quran and find out which verses, if any, support the cause of an Islamic state.

Hundreds of Verses in the Quran are About the Attributes of Allah and the Stories of the Prophets

The attributes of God (the symbol of oneness and the doer of all actions) and stories of the prophets are stated in hundreds of verses in the Quran.

How could the rulers of the North Sudan (a self-declared Islamic state) and the advocates of the Islamic constitution from all over the world, make out from such a huge number of verses, a constitution or a law, while taking into account the fact that these Quranic verses either relate to the attributes of God, or to stories of the noble prophets and their great deeds and miraculous achievements?

Following this same reasoning, let us look at the throne verse (Ayat Al-Kursi) in Arabic, which is a verse in the Quran describing eternal life and the vastness of the throne of God, and the unity in diversity, or consider the luminous light of Allah, which the Quran described in a wonderful similitude: *'Like a niche within which there is a lamp, the lamp is within a glass, the glass as if it were a pearly white planet'* (Alnoor: 35) Is it conceivable that one −however competent− can turn all that majestic glory into constitution or law?

Furthermore, consider the amazing story of the cow of the children of Israel! Consider Solomon's hoopoe, which speaks like a wise person, the intelligent she-camel of Prophet Saleh, the wakeful dog of the companions of the cave (the seven sleepers), the serpent of Moses, or the donkey of the man who came by a ruined village, and exclaimed: How can God bring these ruins to life! So, the man died, and was returned to life a hundred years later! How can one carve all these miracles into a constitution or law?

Under no circumstances can the miraculous story of Prophet Moses, or the story of Prophet Mohammed ascending to the heights of the Heavens, be reduced to a constitution or a law.

The same logical deductions shall apply without exception to the host of stories mentioned in the Quran, for example: Noah's flood, Joseph and his brothers, Moses and the Pharaoh and Jonah and the whale.

Hundreds of Verses of the Quran Speak About the Horrors of Doomsday, the Attributes of Paradise and Hell, the Angels, Satan, the Fairies (Jinn), the News of the Exalted Spiritual Assembly and the Lights of God Abode

Without going into further details about the verses, one can conclude that the above– mentioned verses can never be a constitution or a law. The exalted Spiritual Assembly, the holy of holiness and the untrodden virgin land (see Surahs Saad, and Al-Ahzab) cannot be governed by our laws, touched by our hands, or tramped by our feet.

The highest realms of the Quran are allegorically a pure new land. It is a land high above our mundane affairs, daily worries, problems with our livelihoods, pains of our poverty and complications concerning the accumulation of our wealth. It is also high above our ownership, acquisition and inheritance of property. It is a land where one can fly without wings with the latent power of the Creator. It is a land, which is trodden by none: *'And He caused you to inherit their land, their homes, their property, and a land trodden by none, and Allah is prevailing over everything'* (Al-Ahzaab: 27)

It goes without saying, that one cannot turn into a constitution or a piece of legislation the rest of the verses of the Quran, which belong to this category; for example: The obscure story of the creation of Adam and Eve, and the Satan luring Adam and Eve to expel them from paradise, the miraculous news of the unseen and the holy of holiness.

Hundreds of Verses of the Quran Describe Nature and the Wonders of Creation

Hundreds of verses of the Quran depict breathtakingly the splendour of nature and the hidden beauty of creation of the heavens and the earth. They are bewitching and mesmerising. Many verses of the Quran are Prophet Mohammed's meditation on the glory of nature, which have been manifested in the rising sun, shining moon, twinkling stars, high mountains, tall trees, wonderful animals, sweet dawns and marvelous nights. Thus, how can one turn the beauty of nature into a constitution or a law?

Hundreds of Verses of the Quran Speak about Prayer, Fasting, Pilgrimage (Hajj) and Islamic Rituals

How can verses indicating acts of worship, rituals, and the relation of women and men with God, be assimilated and folded into a constitution or a law to be discussed and passed by parliaments and legal institutions?

Twenty Nine (29) Verses of the Quran are Shortened Intermittent Alphabets

Anyone who peruses the Quran will immediately notice that twenty nine verses are mere shortened intermittent alphabets, which do not bear or reflect any meaning in the Arabic language.

Again, how can the shortened intermittent alphabet verses like: Ha, Meem, Kaf, Ain, Sa-ad, Alif, Lam Ra-a, Noon and Quaf be incorporated into a constitution or legal codes? Actually, in the Quran there are fourteen (14) shortened intermittent alphabet letters in twenty nine (29) verses. In each verse it is indicated that these alphabet letters are the essence of the Quran: *'Alif, Lam, Meem * That is the Book (the Quran)'* (Al-Bagara: 1&2). While this verse indicates very clearly that the shortened intermittent alphabets are the Quran, other similar verses implicate the same in an obscure and fabulous manner. The meaning of these Arabic letters perplexed and agitated the minds of past generations of Muslims, who dared to interpret and issue commentaries on the Holy Quran. It is still a seemingly unsurmountable challenge for Muslim commentators of our current epoch. As a result, the best interpreters among Muslims confined themselves to the uttering: (God alone knows what He means).

One can safely conclude that there are thousands of verses, which are irrelevant to the Islamic government cause and impossible to implement and apply as a constitution or a law. Consequently, propagators of Islam shall –if possible– be honest, and declare to the world that they want to apply only very few verses from the Quran. The applicability of those very few verses is definitely questionable, for the simple reason that they are not deemed fit to be adopted as laws and regulations in any governmental or administrative system.

What is Left from the Verses of the Quran?

The few remaining verses of the Quran address the following issues:
- Verses on Jihad (holy war) and its consequences, including slavery and Jizya (monetary penalty imposed on people of the Book (Jews and Christians) by way of humiliation to confirm that they are second class citizens.
- Verses on Zakat (fixed annual amount of alms calculated and distributed on certain terms and conditions).

- Verses on usury.
- Verses referring to Allah as the Supreme Ruler of the universe.
- Verses referring to men's guardianship over women, succession and distribution of hereditaments.
- Verses mentioning the limits of Allah and the boundaries of His supreme abode.
- Verses interpreted in Sunnah as penalties for violation of the limits of Allah (Hudood).

All these remaining verses may be understood, or rather misunderstood, to support a system of governance, laws and legislations, i.e. an Islamic state. In the Arabic edition of this book, there is a detailed critical study of these verses. There, it is outlined that applying these few verses without really understanding what they are pointing to in essence (Taweel), will lead to catastrophic results. For example, implementing Jihad requires distribution of spoils, slavery of women (termed in the Quran as 'maa malakat Aymanakum', a term repeated fifteen times in fifteen verses) and men, Jizya and humiliation of Christians and Jews, discrimination against women, cruel and inhumane penalties of Hudood (limb amputations), denial of freedom of thought (apostasy legislations) and freedom of expression, etc.

All of these anticipated catastrophic results have been demonstrated by a living example after the declaration of ISIS. Therefore, there is no need to translate all these verses here, or demonstrate how they are understood and applied (as was detailed in the Arabic version of the book). It is now clear to the world that the Islamic state advocates have nothing to offer other than violence and brutality. Ultimately, they represent a serious threat to world peace. It is obvious that without a new and enlightened understanding of the Quran, there is nothing to stand between the Islamists and the total collapse of human civilisation, and possibly the extinction of the human race. That is how serious the current situation is.

Renewal of Islam is an Urgent Necessity

It is clear, therefore, that the Islamists are only really relying on a few verses, amongst thousands, to justify their cause. This, in itself, is a sufficient reason to discard their call, since one cannot justifiably rely on a small part of the Book and ignore the rest of it. The crucial question becomes: How will Muslims, and the rest of the world, face up to these few verses?

It does not help Muslims to simply declare that the violence of ISIS and similar groups is mere extremist action, and that ISIS does not represent Islam. This would be an escapist devise to avoid facing the real challenges represented by those clear Quranic verses however few they may be.

Facing this issue, and rising up to the challenge, requires honesty and courage. Muslims are required to recognise, and admit directly, that the application of these verses leads to violence, discrimination against women and a real threat to freedom. Non-Muslims, on the other hand, while they see and understand the threat of Sharia to fundamental rights, prefer to flatter Muslims, repeating along with Muslims, that Islam is a religion of peace, and describing ISIS and others as mere extremists. However, pretence and flattery will not succeed in averting the problem. The question of facing the Quranic text will still remain unanswered.

The problem must be faced directly. There should be recognition of the shortcomings of Sharia and the disastrous consequences of its application. The traditional Muslim schools of thought are unable to face this dilemma or offer a solution, since most of them do not even recognise that there is a problem. They are content with this state of contradiction manifested by ISIS and similar groups.

Islam renewed is the answer. There is a need for major reforms in Islamic law (Sharia). Not only this, but Islam itself needs renewal and purification from violence, inequality and discrimination. The renewal of Islam depends on the 'Taweel' of the Quran. Taweel, as referred to previously, is the inner, subtle meaning of the words. It is the essence of the Quran. Every word in the Quran carries implications and significance deeper than what is indicated by the literal meaning of the language. Through Taweel, it is possible to understand that the words of the Quran have four dimensions. This understanding will pave the way for solving the apparent contradiction, which is causing the dilemma in which Muslims live today. With Taweel, Islam ceases to be a religion in the usual meaning of the word. It becomes a spiritual aspiration for truth, through purification of the self. These four dimensions, and their significance in the spiritual renaissance in Islam are explained in chapter six (6) of this book.

In the light of Taweel, the few verses used to support the Islamic state concept, will take a completely new meaning. For example the meaning of Jihad will move from fighting outside enemies to going within and fighting the real enemy inside the self. Our real enemies inside the self are fear, sorrow, greed, envy, jealousy, cruelty, etc. In Taweel, there is no Jihad against others whatsoever. The real Jihad, to which the Quran is pointing, is this Jihad within the self. The rest of the words used by Islamists to support their case equally have new and more logical meanings, seen in the light of Taweel.

The duty of the modern state is to serve its citizens and provide for their welfare. It is expected to legislate and execute in diversified ways. Above all, a modern state is responsible for the preservation of public order, security of its citizens and protection of public and private property. All these tasks do not need an Islamic law or an Islamic state. They can competently be accomplished by the human mind and effort, and are open to change every day. It is impossible to classify state regulations and laws into Islamic and non-Islamic laws. Is it conceivable, for example, to find a country with an Islamic Traffic Law and a Non-Islamic one?

In conclusion, there is no support in the Quran for the establishment of an Islamic state. The claim that the Quran calls for an Islamic state is baseless. The Islamists are ignoring the vast majority of the Quran, and relying on a few verses, which they claim support their cause. These few verses in fact refer to a totally different meaning than is currently understood by most Muslims.

In the light of Taweel, the Quran will appropriately resolve the apparent conflict caused by traditional misunderstanding. Islam renewed is the only answer. Taweel is the only answer.

THE FALLACY OF THE ISLAMIC STATE

Chapter 4

The Islamic State a False Idea with no Support in the Sunnah (Sayings and Actions of the Prophet)

The Great Prophet of Islam was not a King, President or a Governor:

The Prophet Mohammed was never addressed by anything other than 'The Prophet' or 'Messenger of Allah', and titles that indicate reverence and illumination. He was looked upon as a teacher and guide to truth. It is an established historical fact that the holy Prophet was given the choice between being a king prophet or a devotee prophet, and that he chose to be a devotee prophet. He chose God, and in the same accord, God chose him. As believed by all Muslims, the almighty associated the Prophet with Him in a lasting and continuous way. It is such a close and intimate relationship, clear and bright.

This exalted attribution is easy to infer from the Quran: 'Immaculate and Glorified is He who took His devotee on a journey by night from the Sacred Mosque to the Farthest Mosque' (Al-Isra': 1). It is further explicitly clarified in this verse: 'When the Devotee of Allah called on Allah'. (Al-Jinn: 19). Also, the Prophet was described as being worthy of praise in this verse: 'Praise be to God, who had sent to His devotee the straight book of illumination' (Al-Kahf: 1). God redeemed the Prophet from darkness through inspiration and realisation of Godhood, in this Quranic phrase: 'The Prophet was as close to God as his own *eyelids, or even closer * Then, God inspired him with that which He inspired * The vision of the heart is certain and unfailing'* (Al-Najm: 9, 10, 11).

Moreover, the Prophet was not praised in the Quran for being a great king or president, but was praised for the nobility of his morals and the integrity of his character. *'Verily, you are of great morals'* (Al-Qalam: 4). The Prophet had never stated that he was sent to establish a kingdom. On the contrary, he stated: 'I have been sent to fulfill the perfection of noble morals'.

Never in his life had the Prophet been addressed by his companions by any title that denotes kingship and/or presidency. The status of the Prophet amongst the people has not been authoritative. The Prophet has been exalted above kingship and presidency. He has been an admonisher and a reminder, not a dominator. *'Therefore do thou remind, for thou art one to remind * Thou art not one to dominate others'* (Al-Ghashiya: 21, 22).

There is no intention to belittle the status of kingship or governance, or to degrade them. The intention is to place the functions of kings and governors in their proper place. Governance, and the exercise of ruling over a population, are civil matters to manage worldly affairs. Proper execution of such functions entails a degree of control and authority. It is similar to managing such activities as agriculture, industry, engineering, medical sciences, trade, etc. However, command and control in matters of administration, judiciary, police and governance is a lot more apparent than in other areas.

It is known that the Prophet had practiced commercial activity to support his family and earn his livelihood during the early days of the message. The ignorant criticised him for doing this, as stated in the Quran: *'And they say, "what sort of apostle is this who eats food and walks in the marketplaces'''?* (Al-Furqan: 7). However, the Prophet abandoned commerce and devoted himself solely to spreading his teachings. The Quran says: *'Did He not find you in need, and enrich you?'* (Ad-Duha: 8).

Then, with the advent of his arrival at the manifest truth, the Prophet placed his full trust upon his lord: *'So put your trust in Allah, for you indeed stand on clear truth'* (An-Naml: 79). He devoted himself wholly to communicating what was revealed to him and to delivering what he was entrusted with. He had executed this in actions, not just words. Had he not done so, he would not have delivered the message: *'O Apostle! Communicate that which has been sent down to you from your Lord, and if you do not, you will not have communicated His message, and Allah shall protect you from the people'.* (Al-Ma'ida: 67). So the lord protected the Prophet from being possessive and/or controlling. He was simply and solely devoted to his mission and always calling for the remembrance of God. The Quran says about the Prophet: *'And you are not one to compel them by force, so remind by the Quran those who fear the premonition '.* (Quaf:45).

Needless to say, the holy Prophet was named by his lord, and people recognise him by hundreds of names, none of which was King, ruler or president. Here are a few examples of the names and titles used for the Prophet: Servant of Allah, Messenger of Allah, Ahmed, Mahmoud, the illuminated light, the bearer of good news, the Caller to Allah, Taha, Yasin, the Good, the Pure, the Trusted, the Honest, the One with Clear Revelation, the Chosen, the Elected, the Companion of God, the Way, the One with a Lofty Status, the Guide, the Guided, the Luminious Light, etc.

Ponder all these names and qualities! Is the title 'King'

among them? Or the title 'governor'?

One Sufi saint described the Prophet thus:
'You are the light of light, who appeared to me,
Even though they call you 'Taha, The Trustworthy'.

It is the great light of the lord, which shone on the face of the noble Prophet because of his surrendering to God. The Quran says: 'The *one whose heart Allah has opened to Islam, has received enlightenment from his Lord'* (Az-Zumar :22)

In this connection, an interesting story may be narrated. It was once said that a Bedouin Arab came to Medina to see the Prophet. When he met the Prophet, he was taken aback by his majestic grandeur. So the Bedouin started stuttering in his speech. The Prophet smiled at the Bedouin and said: 'Relax. I am not a king. I am but a son of an average ordinary woman from the tribe of Quraish, who used to diet on dry meat (AlQuadeed)'.

Why was the Prophet always affirming that he was not a king? He used to say to his companions: 'Do not glorify me as the Romans glorified their kings for I am a servant who sits as a servant, and eats as a servant'.

The Great Prophet of Islam did not Organise Government Offices, State Courts or Promulgate Codes of Law

If the Islamic state was a religious obligation, without which the religion cannot be considered complete, then the Prophet would have established courts, organised government offices and announced himself as king or emperor, or at least as a ruler.

Let there be no confusion over whether these institutions were known at the time. Roman courts were merely a stone's throw away from Yathrib/Medina. The noble Prophet had also visited the land of the Levant several times. In addition, the stories of kings and states are extensively covered throughout the holy Quran.

Why had the Prophet not ordered for the establishment of prisons to house criminals, while the prison of Pharaoh is mentioned in the Quran? Why had he not announced orders and decrees whilst being fully aware of Roman and Persian Emperors? Even average Arabs contemporary to Mohammed were familiar with these two empires.

Why had the Prophet not promulgated Islamic codes of law despite Hammurabi establishing codes of law before the birth of Christ? No one can argue that the noble Prophet was unaware of this, especially as the holy Quran mentions the Hammurabi time and his land in the dialogue between Prophet Abraham and the King.

The Prophet did not adopt a code of law, or establish any of the above-mentioned institutions for the simple reason that there was no system of governance in Islam.

The Islamic State is neither a Religious Obligation, nor a Pillar of Islam

If the Islamic state was a religious duty, then the Prophet would not have hesitated in including it as one of the pillars of Islam as he did with the declaration of faith, prayers, Zakat (giving of alms), fasting and pilgrimage. The Prophet did not do this because there is no system of government in Islam.

What is the Form of the Alleged Islamic Government?

It is known in the principles of constitutional law and political science, that there are different forms of systems, governments and states. One cannot find a trace of that type of description in the Islamic religion, because no system of government exists in Islam.

Had there been an Islamic state, the Prophet would have illustrated a method for selecting the Head of State, but he did not. This is a matter that would not be missed by any average politician, let alone the Prophet with his prudence and intelligence, insight and illuminated prophecy.

Due to the fact that there was no illustrated method for selecting a Head of State, the companions differed on this matter in a disgraceful manner, even before they had cleansed their hands of the dust of the grave of the holy Prophet! Is it conceivable that the companions would differ on this matter, had their Prophet outlined it?

While the Prophet was on his deathbed, the Ansar had said to the Muhajirun: 'From you a prince and from us a prince!', meaning that it was a civil matter to be resolved, so let there be a prince from Al-Muhajirun and another from Al Ansar. Basically, they were saying 'let us appoint our own ruler, and you can appoint yours'. This was said because there was no one ruler expected to govern all Muslims in any prescribed way.

If Khilaapha was a religious matter, or was one of the pillars of Islam, then the Ansar of the messenger of Allah would not have made the above suggestion. The Ansar, being the regiment of Islam and supporters of the Prophet, were praised in the Quran: *'And those who were the landlords, firmly settled in faith, before them [the Ansar], shower their love to whoever migrates to them, and do not find in their heart any deprivation of what is given to them, but prefer (the Muajireen) - to themselves'* (Al-Hashr: 9).

None of the Ansar, the leadership of the Prophet's companions, or those who had been closest to the Prophet, none of them expressed any clear statement from the Prophet regarding what would happen with the matter of governance or political leadership after his departure. In particular, none of them referred to any requirement that a religious state or government was to be established. This is the reason for their disagreement and the ensuing wars.

How did the Noble Prophet Address his Contemporary Kings and Emperors? Did he Request that they Establish an Islamic State?

It is fortunate that historians had preserved some of the letters that the Prophet had sent to his contemporary kings. These letters are authentic and stamped with the Prophet's seal. Reading these letters, it is evident how courteous and appropriate his words were. He gave the kings their proper titles in a manner that suited their esteemed position as leaders of their people.

He had addressed Heraclius as 'The Roman's Great', as narrated by the Islamic historian Ibn Hajar Al Asgalani. There was no invitation in the said letter for the establishment of an Islamic state. On the contrary, the Prophet prayed that the lord would sustain Heraclius' kingship and said to him 'I invite you with the call of Islam'; he also cited this verse: 'Say, O People of the Book!

Come to a righteous word between us and you' (Al-Imran: 64). The Prophet invited the King to embrace Islam, since this was the reason behind the prophetic delegation - he had not asked for anything beyond that.

The noble Prophet also addressed Cyrus (Coptic vicegerent in Egypt) and Kisra of Persia in the same manner. In his letter to Kisra, the Prophet stated: 'I invite you with the call of Allah, as I am the messenger of Allah to all people'. He never referred to himself by any title other than the 'messenger or of Allah'. The Prophet was not an invader, a tax collector or a king. He has been the messenger of guidance for the religion of truth.

The Prophet began his letter to the Negus of the Kingdom of Aksum (present day Ethiopia), with praise for Jesus, the soul of God and the Virgin Mary. He then confined his letter to gentle, concise advice: 'accept my advice'. Is there any reference in these letters to an Islamic state? And is it possible that the messenger of Allah would not refer to it in his letters to Kings and Emperors who are obviously not adhering to an Islamic state (if any)? The Prophet addressed Almunthir Ibn Al-Harith of Damascus in the same way, saying only: 'May the Lord sustain your kingship' and wrote to Ibn Sawi, the governor of Bahrain, saying: 'I will leave what is in your hands as it is'.

You are More Knowledgeable about your Worldly Affairs

In a reported story, the Prophet was once asked about the pollination of palm trees. The Prophet responded in a famous Hadith, saying: 'You are more knowledgeable about your worldly affairs'. It is clear from this Hadith that worldly matters (in this case planting and agricultural activity) are not religious matters.

This surely indicates that the issue of governance and political rule was a civil affair and did not fall within the sphere of religious affairs.

Religious and spiritual knowledge requires insight and an illuminated vision, which can only be attained through divine inspiration. *'Thus we have revealed to you the spirit of our order (highest order) as you were not aware of the meaning of the book or the meaning of belief... It is (book and belief) manifested as a light, through which we guide whom we ever wish)'* (Shoora: 52). The Quran further states: *'He embues the Spirit of His order upon whomever He wishes'* (Ghaafir: 15).

Thus, the state is a worldly matter and people are knowledgeable about worldly affairs. This principle is set very clearly in this Hadith. Furthermore, the Prophet intended to teach his companions lessons in trusting and reliance upon God. However, the general meaning of the Hadith covers all worldly matters discussed above. Read again: 'You are more knowledgeable about your worldly affairs/matters'. Is this not a very clear statement? So, from where does the confusion between human-controlled worldly affairs and spiritual affairs arise?

There are many reasons for this confusion, mainly:

Firstly:The ramifications and consequences of Jihad, like any other war, obliged the Prophet to carry out administrative roles, similar to those of a governor, such as: commanding armies, distribution of spoils and supervising the welfare of the orphans, the widowed, the displaced, the injured and those affected by the war.

Secondly: The establishment of certain penalties for certain offenses, commonly known in Sunnah as 'Hudood'.

Thirdly: Some prophets assumed administrative roles, while some were rulers and kings.

Each of these points will be clarified as follows:

Prophet Mohammed Lays Down the Religious Foundation for the Cancellation of Jihad 'Holy War'

Jihad is a transitional and temporary system. It is reported that Prophet Mohamed used to repeat at the end of each battle: 'We have returned from the smaller Jihad to the greater Jihad', meaning that they have returned from the physical outer Jihad, to the inner Jihad of the self.

The words of the Quran are laid down at four different levels. The first level deals with the universe (outer physical existence), the second level deals with the self (inner consciousness). The third level is about seeing things as they are (truth). The fourth level is the continuous witnessing and realisation of truth as demonstrated in the Quran. *'We will show them our signs on the horizon and within themselves, till they clearly realise that it is the truth, was it not sufficient that your Lord is the witness who observes everything'.* (Fussilat: 53).

Each word in the Quran has a particular meaning at each of these four levels. This insight is confirmed by the Quran thus: *'He is the First and the Last, the Apparent and the Hidden'* (Alhadeed: 3). Depending on this understanding, Sufi saints interpreted the verse: *'Fight the closest non-believers to you'* (Al-Touba: 123) to mean: fight your enemies within, who are closest to you. The five senses are the closest inner enemy because they are limited and create a veil between man and God. This is a subtle meaning for the word 'non-believers' mentioned in the verse. However, there are many deeper meanings. Detailed explanation of these various levels of the Quran has been offered in our other publications.

Some Muslim scholars and thinkers made efforts to cancel Jihad (for example, the Qadianis, and Baha'is). However, these efforts were mostly superficial and pre-mature as they lacked depth and comprehensive knowledge of the Quran. These scholars failed to see the hidden wisdom behind the words. The Muslim sage Ustadh Mahmoud Mohammed Taha succeeded in promulgating a sound interpretation of the Quran that cancels Jihad. Ustadh Mahmoud was aware that his message required further elaboration and evolution as was clear from his writings.

The significant point to be confirmed is that Prophet Mohamed himself had already established the foundation for the cancelation of Jihad at the end of each battle, as pointed out in his above Hadith. Moreover, the Prophet never personally participated in battle or used a sword. If Jihad had been a pillar of Islam, then Prophet Mohammed himself would have certainly participated in it.

In his last sermon at the conquest of Mecca, the Prophet revealed the transitional and temporary nature of Jihad. He stated: 'Mecca is sanctified by God, not by people. He who believes in God and the Hereafter, is not allowed to shed blood in Mecca. This has been so before me, and shall continue to be so after me. I was only permitted to make an exception at this hour. Therefore, no blood shall be shed, nor a tree cut. If anyone sheds blood relying on the Prophet's permission to wage war, let them know that God gave permission to His messenger, not to them. Only the messenger is permitted for an hour of this day. Today, the sanctity of Mecca is confirmed as it was yesterday. So, he who witnesses my words, shall convey the same to those who are absent'. The complete text of the last sermon is documented in many sources including the famous Ibn Hisham biography of the Prophet. The permission referred to here by the Prophet is corroborated by the Quran: *'It is not you who slew them, it is God who slew them. You did not caste, but God casted'*. (Al-Anfaal: 17). In other words, the Prophet was not acting out of his personal volition, and his companions only implemented God's will, as is clear from the verse: *'It is God who slew them'.*

By stating clearly that 'permission' was restricted exclusively to the Prophet, no Muslim can rely on the Prophet's actions to propagate Jihad. The Prophet acted according to his insight and divine vision. The Quran states: *'In order to rule amongst the people as shown to you by God'*. (Al-Nisaa: 105). Even at this level, the Prophet had an option to rule or not to rule. The Quran says: *'Rule amongst them, or abstain'.* (Al-Maida: 42). This is satisfactory proof that there is no Islamic state. If an Islamic State was an obligation, it is not conceivable that the Prophet would have a choice.

Moreover, the Arabic word for 'rule' is not derived from 'governance', but it refers to the will of God, or divine vision. Clearly the Prophet acted according to divine vision. It goes without saying that the propagators of the Islamic state neither have the spiritual eye nor the divine vision.

It is well-known that the sanctity of Mecca is based on the location of the sacred mosque (and the Ka'aba), which is the direction of prayer. At the same time, the Prophet had stated: 'All the earth is made a sacred mosque for me'. Therefore, the cancellation of Jihad in Mecca is paving the way for cancelling it on the whole earth.

Furthermore, the Quran considers God to be present everywhere. The Quran states *'He (God) is with you wherever you are'*. (Al-Hadeed: 4). The Quran also considers that the face of God is all prevailing. It reads: *'Wherever you turn, there is the face of God'* (Al-Bagara: 115). Accordingly, the direction of prayer in

Islam is everywhere. But this can only be seen through the light of the heart of those who accept the will of God. *'We may see the turning of your face towards the heavens, we will guide you in the direction of contentment'* (Al-Bagara: 144).

If one listens attentively to the last sermon of the Prophet, he will understand clearly that the Prophet has been paving the way for the irrevocable and unconditional abolition of bloodshed anywhere and at any time. In Islam only the Prophet was permitted to declare Jihad. Even the Prophet was allowed to do so only at a certain hour, in a certain place, and in particular circumstances, which had ceased to exist immediately after his death.

It is worth noting that some of the companions of the Prophet were very attentive as the Prophet delivered this last sermon. One of these companions stated: 'I was listening to the Prophet attentively with my ears, eyes and heart'. The meaning of this last sermon, if properly understood, was that no Muslim would be excused in declaring Jihad. The declaration of Jihad was solely restricted to the Prophet for the reasons mentioned above.

Prophet Mohammed Lays the Religious Foundation for the Cancellation of 'Al-Hudood'

Al-Hudood is the Arabic word for 'limitations'. It should be noted that this word 'Hudood' has never been mentioned in the Quran in relation to criminal penalties. However, the word has been defined by Islamic jurists to mean criminal penalties. This definition was based on certain statements of the Prophet.

It is significant to point out that Prophet Mohammed said: 'Avert 'Hudood' on the basis of the least doubt'. This statement of the Prophet really means: 'cancel' the Hudood. The Prophet used the Arabic word 'Adra'aoo', translated here as 'avert'. This word 'Adra'aoo' is consistently used in the Quran in five different verses to mean remove and cancel - in the Surahs of: Al-Baqara Al-Umran Ar-Ra'd Al-Noor, and Al-Qasas.

The outstanding Sunni jurist Abu Hanifa Al-Nua'amaan was very flexible in his interpretation of the Prophet's expression 'the least doubt'. Abu Hanifa stated that if one is accused of theft, and claims without proof that the stolen property is his own, his hand should not be cut off. Abu Hanifa was of the opinion that in such cases, even without proof, the accused should be given the benefit of the doubt in accordance with the Prophet's statement.

This flexibility in interpretation by Abu Hanifa is derived from the teachings of Imam Ja'afar Alsadiq, who is the founder of Shia'at jurisprudence. In other words there is a consensus between the two leading Muslim schools of thought on this point.

Giving the accused the benefit of the doubt is an established legal principle. It is also a required principle from a religious and logical perspective. This is because an error made to pardon is better than one made to convict, and it is better to forgive one hundred guilty persons than to indict one innocent person. As Thomas Jefferson put it: 'It is better to set a hundred guilty men free, than jail one innocent man'. The point is evidently clear. For those familiar with criminal law, and the laws of evidence, they will be aware that doubt does arise to some degree in almost every criminal case.

Comments on Prophets who Assumed Some Administrative Roles

From the very beginning it is significant to confirm that the kingdom of the prophets is the kingdom of wisdom and knowledge. The Quran says: *'We have granted the people of Abraham the Book and the wisdom, and we granted them a great kingdom'* (Al-Nissa: 54). However, this great kingdom can only be seen if one looks twice, deeply and meditatively. The Quran says: *'If you looked and looked; you will see bliss and a great kingdom'* (Al-Insaan: 20). For this reason, the austere great Sufi, Ibrahim Ibn Adham, said: 'We live in such ecstasy, that if it is known by kings, they would fight us over it with swords'.

It is to be noted that the leading prophets who attained great spiritual heights, namely: Noah, Abraham, Moses, Jesus and Mohammed were never kings. They were only instructed to promulgate religious directives from the one religion, as stated in the Quran: *'He promulgated for you, from the same religion, that which He enjoined on Noah, and that which We have inspired to you, and that which We enjoined on Abraham, Moses and Jesus, namely: that you should remain steadfast in religion and make no division there in. Your call is too high for the dualist, and God chooses to Himself those whom He will, and guide those who turn to Him'* (Al-Shoora:13).

Teaching and guiding their people to the right path occupied such great prophets. They did not have time for mundane affairs such as kingdoms. It is of significant importance to notice that the verse did not refer to religions, but was referring to 'the religion'. At such high spiritual levels religion is one. It is the religion of surrender to the supreme God. This process of surrendering is Islam. The Quran says: *'Whoever aspires to a religion other than Islam, will not be accepted from him'* (Al-Imran: 85). The same meaning is confirmed in the verse: *'The religion at the abode of God is Islam'* (Al-Imran: 19).

At this level, the religion of Islam existed before Mohammed. Abraham was a Muslim, as were Moses and Jesus. The Quran says: *'The prophets who surrendered to the will of God'* (Al-Ma'ida: 44), and: *'We were Muslims before him (Mohammed)"* (Al-Gassas: 53). Islam here does not refer to dogmas or rituals, but to a natural surrender to the higher will that governs all the cosmos. Islam in this sense has no relationship with the violence, chaos or confusion spread nowadays by militant Muslims.

However, there are some prophets, who had spiritually supported some kings, for a certain purpose and for a limited time. As stated in the Quran: *'their prophet said to them: God had sent Tallut as King over you'.* (Al-Bagara: 247).

The statement that great prophets were not kings does not mean that some other prophets did not assume the roles of kings, for transitional periods and for certain reasons. David assumed a king's role, when he attained the status of Al-Khalifa. *'Oh David, We made thee vicegerent (Khalifa) on earth, then rule the people by virtue of the truth'* (Saad: 26).

It is to be noticed that the verse stated 'rule the people by virtue of the truth' and did not refer to a certain legislation or Sharia. This is due to the fact that there is no religious government with a definite form or mandate; instead, truth is descended to earth at various levels from day to day. Not withstanding his high status, David was unable to arrive at the right decision in the case of the field and the goats as narrated in the Quran. However his son Solomon was able to understand the case better than his father. The Quran says: *'We have given Solomon the understanding of the matter, and We granted both (David and Solomon) knowledge and high order'* (Al-Anbia': 78). This understanding of the order of things is the true knowledge. Prophet Mohammed used such true knowledge to be a devotee prophet not a king prophet. The mere fact that Prophet Mohammed had the choice to be either a devotee prophet or a king prophet, shows that there are two levels. The higher level is a devotee prophet and the lower level is a king prophet. The fact that Prophet Mohammed had chosen to be a devotee prophet is satisfactory proof that there is no kingdom or religious government in Islam.

The statement that there is no religious government in Islam does not mean that civil governments are secluded from seeking guidance in religious principles. On the contrary, civil governments may apply the values of justice and truth, which are stated in the Quran, sacred scriptures and in many other books of wisdom and jurisprudence. This point will be elaborated on further in chapter five of this book.

The expression 'there is no religious government in Islam' means that there is no such thing in Islam as a religious government, with a certain form, presided over by a Khilafa or any other corresponding title. The status of Al-Khilafa is a spiritual status granted by God as stated in this verse: *'We made thee vicegerent (Khalifa)'* (Saad: 26).

In Islam, no one has the right to assume the role of Khilafa and demand the people's allegiance to himself.

The greatest upheaval in Islam (the Great Fitna) happened when the companion of Mohammed, Osman Ibn Affan, refused to resign from Khilafa claiming: 'I will not take off a robe tailored for me by God'. The result of the Fitna was the death of many people, including Osman himself. The bloodshed continued all through the ages whenever the Khilafa is declared. The most recent examples are Abubakr Baghdadi of ISIS and Bashir of Sudan.

Supporting the 'non-existence' of a religious government in Islam is the story of Joseph –a high status prophet–who was appointed in charge of the treasury by the king of Egypt (a role similar to a Minister of Finance). Noticeably, Joseph did not say to the king that his government was a non-religious one. He simply offered his qualifications to perform the duties assigned to him without ever mentioning that he was a prophet. The Quran says: *'He (Joseph) said: Appoint me in charge of the treasures of the earth, I am an all-knowing keeper'.* (Yousif: 55). So, the king appointed Joseph as a minister, and he was one of the king's greatest ministers. Thus, a knower of the truth or a prophet can assume any position according to qualification, competence, knowledge honesty, trustworthiness, truthfulness and just behaviour, like any other competent employee.

It is well-known that the prophet David was a blacksmith and a musician. Noah was a carpenter, Jesus was a carpenter apprentice, Mohammed was a shepherd and merchant and Solomon was a king. This does not mean, however, that there is such a thing as religious blacksmithing, religious music, religious carpentry, religious commerce or a religious kingdom.

THE FALLACY OF THE ISLAMIC STATE

Chapter
5

The Islamic State Through the Ages

The Islamic State in the Past

In the previous chapters, the concept of an Islamic state was shown to be false and baseless in the light of the Quran and the Sunnah of the Prophet.

In this chapter, we will consider the Islamic state in its various manifestations and names, both in the past and in our present time. We will look at specific examples, starting with the period of the righteous Caliphs, which is considered by Muslims to be the golden age of the Islamic state. We will then shed some light on how these forms of the Islamic state developed. This will confirm yet again that, throughout history, attempts to force this false concept on society inevitably resulted in violence, bloodshed, anarchy and violation to the rule of law.

How did Abu Bakr's Caliphate Commence?

People paid allegiance to Abu Bakr in Saqifa Bani Saidah, without the presence of a large number of leading companions, namely: Ali Ibn Abi Talib, Al-Zubair Ibn Awwam and Abdullah Bin Abbas. Also, most of the Muhajireen and Ansar were not present.

It is known in Islamic history that Ali Ibn Abi Talib refused to pledge allegiance to Abu Bakr for an entire six months. He only paid allegiance after the departure of Fatima, his wife and the daughter of the Prophet. Ali's acceptance of Abu Bakr's Caliphate is justified by Ali's desire to avert bloodshed, as will be revealed later. Likewise, Fatima, the daughter of the Prophet had abstained from giving allegiance to Abu Bakr until her death. Not only this, but she recommended that neither Abu Bakr nor Omar should attend at her burial prayers if she was to pass away; this recommendation was carefully implemented by Ali.

Abu Bakr was selected for Khilaapha amidst an atmosphere of increased confusion, disagreement and loud voices, as the historian Ibn Hisham tells us in his biography of the Prophet. Abu Bakr was chosen by a minority, in the absence and/or disagreement of the majority. Fortunately, the majority of the companions preferred not to fight with Abu Bakr. According to Omar Ibn Al-Khattab, Abu Bakr became a Caliph by mere chance, or as he put it in Arabic 'a falta', i.e. a slip. Omar stated: 'Abu Bakr's allegiance was a 'falta', that God prevented people from its possible evil consequences'.

As prophethood cannot be inherited, the companions were not sure about what Abu Bakr's title was. For example, a companion once addressed Abu Bakr by saying: 'Oh Caliph of Allah'; Abu Bakr responded: 'That is Jesus the son of Mary'. In the end it was agreed that he should be addressed as the Caliph of the Prophet. Omar was addressed as the 'Caliph of the Caliph of the Prophet'. It is clear that this title was not going to be practical for subsequent Caliphs. Therefore, Omar chose the title: 'The Prince of the Believers' (Emir Al-Muminin). Of course, the title prince (Emir) is a civil term for one who administers government affairs.

Whatever the case may be, the Caliphate was a heavy burden for Abu Bakr. As was indicated earlier, it got to a point where Omar had suggested to Abu Bakr to burn Ali and Fatima alive for their refusal to recognise his rule. That is where Abu Bakr made his statement referred to earlier: 'Take your Caliphate from me and give me back my religion'. This incident triggered the following response from the Poet of the Nile, the famous Hafiz Ibrahim, articulating Omar's statement in his poetry:

'I will burn your house,

Together with the daughter of the Prophet,

If you do not pledge allegiance, at the moment'

What kind of an Islamic state can any Muslim build, on the ashes of the burned body of the Prophet's beloved daughter?

In fact, allegiance in Islam can only be pledged to God alone. The Quran states that very clearly: '*Verily those who pledge allegiance to thee are pledging allegiance to God*'. (Al-Fath: 10). That is because in Islam, obedience to the Prophet is obedience to God. The Quran says: '*He who obeys the Messenger, obeys Allah*'. (Al-Nisa': 80)

Omar's Reign

As it happened, Abu Bakr was not comfortable with shouldering the Khilaapha responsibility, and its consequences. Before his death, Abu Bakr appointed Omar as his successor to avoid anticipated conflict. No Shoora proceedings were followed, and no one was in fact consulted at all about Omar's appointment. Had Abu Bakr known that Shoora (consultation) was the binding method, he would have been obliged to apply it. It is inconceivable that a man of Abu Bakr's stature would deliberately violate explicit religious instructions.

In the same way, Omar himself did not apply the Shoora process. He appointed six men to choose a successor from amongst themselves. He excluded all the Ansar (Prophet's supporters) from Al-Aws & Khazraj, the main residents of the Caliphate capital city, and the owners of its land. He also excluded many leading companions of the Prophet, including Abdalla Ibn Abbas, who was considered by the Prophet as the scholar of the nation and the interpreter of the Quran. Also, Ammar Ibn Yasir who was promised heaven by the Prophet, was excluded. Even worse, Omar ordered the beheading of any of the elected six if he disagreed with the choice of the rest. That is how Omar chose to deal with the matter of Khilaapha after him. Is it possible to claim that there was any freedom in choosing a Caliph?

In the light of the above historical facts, it is not plausible to claim that the behavior of Abu Bakr and Omar with respect to succession was a mere misapplication of a religious principle. In fact, there exists no such principle or theory, because there is no religious government in Islam.

Moreover, and assuming for the sake of argument that Shoora (which is used by Islamists as the basis for the claim for an Islamic state) is indeed a religious requirement set for choosing a Caliph, it must be pointed out that the result of any Shoora is not binding. The Quran gives the Prophet the right to consult, and gives him the right to final decision irrespective of the result of the Shoora. The Quran left the final decision to the determination of the Prophet, and not to the opinion of his companions: *'And when thou has taken a decision, then put thy trust in Allah'* (Al-Imran: 159).

In addition, the Quran requires Shoora only from the Prophet, in relation to his dealings with the companions in a gentle and merciful manner, full of forgiveness. The Quran says: *'It is part* of the Mercy of Allah that thou deals gently with them' (Al-Imraan: 159). Moreover the Quran instructs the Prophet to waive their error, pardon and seek forgiveness for them and ease their thoughts by consulting with them: *'So pass over (their faults), and ask for (Allah's) forgiveness for them; and consult with them in affairs'* (Al-Imran: 159).

The success of Omar's Caliphate is mostly attributed to civil and administrative reasons. Omar did not choose his assistants and governors on the basis of religious grounds. He had inaugurated Amr Ibn Al-'as as the governor of Egypt despite Amr's bitterest animosity with the Prophet during the early days of Islam. In the same way, Omar appointed Muawiyah Ibn Abi Sufyan over The Levant (present-day Syria and Lebanon); Muawiyah and his immediate family had been strong opponents of the Prophet.

Omar gave the largest regions of the land of Islam at the time to be ruled by the least 'religious' amongst the companions. He did not appoint people of precedence in Islam, or those who memorised the holy Quran. It is clear that Omar was conscious that he was managing a civil state, which required capable and efficient administrators. Therefore, he did not use religious criteria for selection. Omar was aware that the Prophet had not appointed a Caliph. Is not Omar the one who said: 'If I do not appoint a successor, then that was done by he who was better than I am - referring to the Prophet - and if I appoint a successor, then this was done by someone better than I am - meaning Abu Bakr'?

So there was no criterion for governance other than civil studiousness and administrative competence. For practical reasons, despite clear Quranic instruction, Omar did not apply these instructions on numerous occasions. For example:

a. Omar did not apply verses granting alms to newly converted Muslims in order to soften their hearts, termed in Arabic 'Al mualafati qulubuhum'

b. Omar issued an order to suspend the application of punishment for theft (hand amputation) during the year of the Ash/famine - 'A'am Alramada'.

c. Omar prohibited marriage for Muslim men to Christian and/or Jewish women in contradiction with clear Quranic verses.

d. Moreover, and without any sanction or support from the Quran, Omar also decided to confine the companions of the Prophet (including Ali Ibn Abi Talib) to Medina only.

It is agreed amongst Islamic historians that Omar ruled with rigour and severity. It was natural therefore, that Omar's reign paved the way for great strife and bloodshed, in which the blood of Muslims was spilled throughout Islamic history. Until this day, whenever the topic of the Islamic government is raised, untold misery, pandemic evil and bloodshed will immediately follow.

The Great Upheaval (Al-Fitna Al-Kubra)

The great upheaval (Fitna) is a time when Muslims beaheaded each other in great wars, which broke immediately after the death of Omar's successor Osman. I do not wish to delve into the details of the bloody events of the great Fitna in this quick overview. It is enough to mention that the battle of Al-Jamal took place between Ali Ibn Abi Talib and the Mother of the Believers, Aisha, supported by Zubair Ibn Awwam and Talha Ibn Obeid Allah. Both of them were leading companions.

The details regarding Ali's subsequent battles against Muawiyah and his broke-away companions, the Khawaarij, were mentioned in chapter 1 of this book, concluding with the extermination of most of the Prophet's companions and the Prophet's own family.

It is clear, therefore, that the companions of the Prophet, and the four first righteous Caliphs of the Prophet, failed to establish an Islamic state. This being that, can the Islamists of today accomplish what the companions of the Prophet failed to do?

The Omayyad and Abbasid Dynasties

After the death of the first Omayyad Caliph, Muawiyah, his son, Yazeed Ibn Muawiyah, inherited power. Yazeed opened his reign by killing Al-Huseein Ibn Ali and seventy of the Prophet's family in one day. Moreover, he killed ten thousand of the Ansar of the Prophet in the battle of That Al-Harra, where he committed massacres in the city of the Prophet. It was genocide against the supporters of the Prophet, who housed, protected and assisted the Prophet to victory.

Regarding the Abbasids, it is enough to note that the first Abbasid Caliph was nicknamed "Al-Saffah", meaning "The Slayer". Also, Al-Mamoon, the greatest of Bani Abbas' Caliphs, had killed his own brother, Al-Ameen. Furthermore, the Caliph Harun Al-Rasheed killed his ministers and supporters from Al-Baramika, who helped establish the Abbasid Empire itself. In the same way, Caliph Abu Jaffar Mansour killed his minister and right-hand-man Abu Muslim Al-Kharasani.

The Turkish Caliphate and other Islamic emirates followed the footsteps of the Omayyads and the Abbasids. Their rule also being marred by violence and bloodshed. It is needless to delve into the rest of these tragedies.

However, the periods of the Omayyads and Abbasids were considered successful in the civil sphere when compared with other kingdoms and empires of the same era. All ancient empires and kingdoms had been established with the shrewdness of politicians and the cunningness of generals, over the remains of the corpses of unknown soldiers. The claimed Islamic state was no exception.

The Islamic State in the Contemporary World – The Sudanese Model

Muslim Brothers seized power in Sudan through a military coup in June 1989, and declared the country to be an Islamic state. In 2011, and as a consequence to the application of Islamic Law and jihad, the Christian Southern part of the country was separated from the North. The President of Sudan or, more accurately, what is left of Sudan, has gone too far in his false call for the establishment of an Islamic government in Northern Sudan. A government that does not recognise the country's cultural and religious diversity, as he affirmed in his city of Ghadarif speech, following the separation of the South. In that speech, he claimed that his government will rule by floggings, amputations and crucifixion.

Further, the president of North Sudan confirmed in his Kabashi Village address that he would establish his Islamic state on the corpses of 'martyrs'. He continued to assert that either Islam's glory returns, or blood be shed in pursuit of it! Thus the first question is: Why has he not succeeded in restoring the glory of Islam in over 20 years of totalitarian rule? The more intriguing question is: Which blood will he now shed? Will it be the blood of the people of North Sudan, for whom he claims to have established peace by separating from South Sudan? This irresponsible claim is not just a slip of the tongue, but a planned plot and an old rhetoric of the president in particular, and of some of his advisors and ministers in general. All of them pretend to embrace democracy and peace by simply preaching it. However, they contradict democracy and carry on with their old habit of promoting violence. The famous Arab poet Al-Mutanabbi says:

'When you act in pretence and against your nature,
You will immediately fall, and reurn to your stature'

The president's irresponsible words reflect the incoming evil of an establishment of an Islamic state in Northern Sudan and the rest of the Islamic world. This rhetoric should not be allowed to pass unchecked, and must be observed carefully. One can legitimately ask: Why had the president of the Islamic government of Sudan declared Jihad on the people of the South, shedding the blood of millions of innocent people? The same president later claimed to have established peace by dividing the country, resembling a failing doctor boasting about healing his patients by killing them! It would have been honourable for the government of Sudan to announce that the idea of Jihad in South Sudan was wrong and woeful, and that the government had returned to the right path by signing the Comprehensive Peace Agreement (CPA). Instead of doing that, the government typically considered its own failure to be a virtue, and continued to boast, positioning itself as the achiever of peace, while carrying on with instigating conflict in Darfur, Blue Nile, South Kordofan and other parts of the country.

The Islamic government of Sudan does not care about the pain of victims' families, nor does it feel a moral, religious or financial obligation towards the hundreds of thousands of victims who

105

sacrificed their lives, lost their livelihoods and whose blood was shed for the sake of the false, void, idea of Jihad against Southerners, all in pursuit of the Islamic state illusion.

To add insult to injury, the president of the Islamic government in Sudan stated in one of his recorded speeches about the war in Darfur, that he did not want to see a prisoner or a wounded person left in the battlefield. In other words, he was saying that he wanted to witness his nation crushed like ants by his soldiers.

The president had thought that his Islamic state dream would be realised after he paved the way for the separation from the South. He insisted on the inclusion of two legal systems within the Comprehensive Peace Agreement. Furthermore, he proceeded with his oppressive, arbitrary policies that restricted freedoms. The president reckoned that by isolating the North, he would be free to degrade and humiliate the people using Sharia law, which blatantly curtails freedom of expression and belief.

These are the same laws that were promulgated by his predecessor General Jafar Numeiri. In September 1983, Numeiri declared Sharia law in Sudan and appointed himself as an Imam for Muslims. He surrounded himself with the Muslim Brotherhood movement and some pseudo Sufi leaders. President Bashir is now following the footsteps of Numeiri.

The Sudanese application of Islamic laws in our contemporary time, confirms that wherever there is a call for Islamic law, bloodshed, violence and arbitrary rule will prevail. There is no need to examine other systems in other countries, which claim to have established an Islamic state. They all face the same dilemma of misunderstanding the Quranic text, and misunderstanding the proper application of the Sunnah of the Prophet. In every example you could think of, including Turkey, Malaysia, Saudi Arabia, Morocco, Jordan, Pakistan, Indonisia, etc, there is a common denominator of contradiction and denial of fundamental rights. The apparent progress in infrastructure, and the seemingly advanced education and economic systems in some of these countries, are due to civil, scientific and secular developments; they have nothing to do with the application of Islamic laws.

THE FALLACY OF THE ISLAMIC STATE

Chapter
6

The Islamic State Concept
Violates Constitutional Principles

What is a Constitution?

A constitution is the fundamental law, which determines the nature and form of a state. It defines and organises state powers, and regulates the relationships between the various authorities and the way in which they are to be instituted. A constitution establishes the fundamental principles for internal governance and determines the tasks assigned to each of the government authorities. It also sets out general guidelines for the procedure to be followed in exercising legislative, judicial and executive powers, and organises the jurisdiction of each authority on its own and in relation to other authorities. In other words, the legislative, judicial and executive powers are separate and cooperative.

A constitution also establishes individual fundamental rights. These are the rights to life, liberty and complete equality without discrimination on the basis of belief, religion, race, gender or colour. A constitution also guarantees fundamental freedoms including the freedom of thought, religion, expression, association and movement. Furthermore, it determines the distribution of sovereign powers within the sovereign state.

Constitutional concepts have evolved and developed all through human history, culminating at the doorstep of the consolidated fundamental principle of 'constitutionality of laws'. This principle means that any legislation issued by any legislative body, whatever name it carries (be it parliament, congress, senate, national assembly, national council, etc.), must be compatible and consistent with the constitution. Otherwise, that legislation will be void, and can be so declared by the courts pursuant to an application by an aggrieved party. Relevant courts, as the custodians and interpreters of the constitution, are, on their own initiative, empowered to decide upon the constitutionality of laws. These powers are exercised according to the procedures and systems adopted in every civilised country that respects the rule of law, where the dignity of an individual and his right to life and freedom are catered for.

The principle of 'constitutionality of laws' also governs the whole structure of legislation at its various levels. Accordingly, all bi-legislations such as regulations, orders, notifications, instructions and rules issued by central or local authorities should all be consistent and in agreement with the law, and thereby with the constitution. Otherwise they are considered null and void, and without effect.

The constitutionality of laws is a modern concept. It did not become reality by mere chance. It is the fruit of the long human struggle for truth, justice and freedom. A lot of blood, sweat and tears have been shed in this long and bitter struggle.

The story of the constitution is the story of this long human effort in the search for truth and justice. This drama can be observed in the conflict between the 'haves' and the 'have-nots', since time immemorial. The seed of the constitution was planted even before Christ was born. It can be traced in some form or another in the Hamorabi Code, the democratic government of Athens, the Encyclopedias of Roman Law, the Tablets of Moses, the Judgments of David and Solomon, etc. The success of these examples have served as motivation for the prevalence of good over evil on earth, helping humanity in its march towards perfection. However, it should be recognised that there is still a long way to go.

The story of the constitution continued to evolve right up until the advent of Islam in the seventh century AD. Islam laid down some management, social and economic regulations known as Islamic Sharia. Sharia in its totality and its detail was an attempt to establish justice in a primitive society. However, it was not based on the spirit of Islam's teachings, which was flowing with forgiveness, equality, justice and perfection. Instead, the regulations for the seventh century human society fell way short of modern-day standards of recognising people's right of freedom and equality. That is why one finds that textbooks on Sharia law talk endlessly of the rules and regulations for slavery, distribution of bounty in Jihad (holy war), and the killing of apostates. Sharia law also regulates in matters such as veiling of women and giving a woman only half the right of a man in testimony and inheritance, one quarter of his right in marriage, or even less than a quarter if she was a slave, etc. These rules would be fairly well-known to anyone with average knowledge of Islamic jurisprudence and history.

The Evolution of Constitutional Thought

The evolution of constitutional thought started slowly but continued more rapidly during the middle ages, where English law saw the birth of the Magna Carta, or 'The Supreme Covenant'. The Magna Carta is a covenant of rights, endorsed by King John of England on 15 June 1215, and consequently approved with some changes by kings Henry the 3rd and Edward the 1st. Jurists consider the Magna Carta to be the basis for English constitutional liberty. This great covenant contains 38 chapters dealing with rules of justice and principles of law enforcement, and defining secular and church jurisdictions, i.e. pointing out the separation of religion from the state. Articles in this covenant also contain sections on personal and political freedom and the right to property ownership for individual citizens; furthermore, they establish stipulated tax obligations, as well as church rights.

The Magna Carta establishes another principle in English law known as the writ of 'Habeas Corpus Ad Subjiciendum'. It is a summons with the force of a court order, requiring a government authority to bring before the court a person in their custody on a specified date, and it explains the reasons. The purpose of the summons is to protect individual freedom and prevent or guard against unlawful detention. There are many forms of Habeas Corpus, but the type we are concerned with here is considered the most important judicial order in the history of English law, hence it is known as the 'Great Writ of Liberty'.

During the time of the renaissance and the enlightenment, the meanings of justice and constitutional values developed further at the hands of many philosophers and thinkers such as Thomas Hobbs, Jean Jack Russo, John Locke and Montesquieu. Their contribution represented an extension and a culmination of Aristotle's thought as laid out in his famous book, 'Politics'.

On 21 June 1788, the American Constitution was ratified. It was codified in a single document, which was influenced greatly by the English constitution, even though the latter was not written in one document. Many other constitution-making experiences followed suit in Europe, Canada, Australia, India, Japan and many other countries all over the world.

Accordingly, it is safe to say that all applicable constitutions in today's world have been subject to development and modernisation. They represent the ripe fruit of humanity's long struggle to come out of the chains of slavery and into the patios of freedom. It was a movement on the ascending path that leads to the elimination and defeat of erroneous thought, where might creates right, towards the birth of correct thought where right creates might. Only then can rights and obligations be decided on the basis of justice, and in accordance with the scales of correct values.

This is the meaning of modern constitution. It is the foundation on which political authority is exercised in present-day democratic countries. However, the governments as well as the people of these countries recognise that they have not yet achieved perfection in applying their constitutions and in realising justice, because there is no end to perfection. Thus, if someone claims that Islamic Sharia, which prevailed many centuries prior to these gigantic developments, is the constitution, or that Sharia is capable of forming the foundation of a constitution, that person is demonstrably ignorant of both the constitution and of Sharia.

It is clear that the idea of the constitution is an evolving experience. This is evident as we observe the developments that took place in the mid 20th century, and the subsequent vital steps taken to recognise human rights internationally, culminating in the adoption of the Universal Declaration of Human Rights, which is signed by United Nations member states, including Sudan.

This is a good point at which to examine the validity (or non-validity) of the concept of an Islamic state in relation to the Universal Declaration of Human Rights.

The Universal Declaration of Human Rights

The Universal Declaration of Human Rights is an international rights document, representing a declaration adopted by the United Nations on 10 December 1948 at the Shibu Palace in Paris. The declaration clarifies the United Nations' view with regards to the protection of human rights for all. The declaration is amongst the most important documents adopted by the UN, occupying a prominent place in international law together with the International Covenant on Civil and Political Rights 1966 and the International Covenant for Economic, Social and Cultural Rights 1966. The three documents have formed the International Bill of Human Rights, which is enforceable by international law.

There is a distinction between human rights law and international humanitarian law. The latter deals with international (and national) armed conflict and regulates relations between armed groups and civilians. This distinction is explained in detail in the various international treaties available and easily accessible to all, thanks to the information technology revolution.

In reviewing the foundation of the major documents mentioned above, we find that the International Covenant on Civil and Political Rights provides for rights relating to self determination, fair trail, equality, life and freedom - including freedom of expression, thought, conscience, religion, peaceful assembly and association; freedom of association includes trade union and political parties' rights. Furthermore, the Covenant protects from torture and degrading and inhumane treatment, slavery and unlawful arrest.

There is no doubt that with a quick review, one will find that in countries where Islamic Sharia is claimed to be applicable, the law stands in stark contradiction with, and is in clear violation of, the International Covenant on Civil and Political Rights. For example, at the theoretical level as well as the practical level, Islamic Sharia allows for slavery, and cruel and degrading treatment. It also allows flogging, amputation of the hand and leg and death by stoning and crucifixion. All of these punishments are practiced with 'cruelty'. These practices are indeed supported by the explicit text in the Quran that reads: *'Retribution and cruelty (in punishment) from Allah'* (Al-Maida: 38).

It is also established that In Sharia, there is no allowance for political parties to be formed. If this were allowed in Sharia, all the disputes between the companions of the Prophet described in this book would not have taken place. Ali Ibn Abi Talib for example, would have been able to create a political party. The Mother of the Believers (Umm Al-Mumineen), Aisha Bint Abi Bakr, would have formed another one in opposition, while Talha and Elzubeir would have been members in her party. If freedom of association was possible in Sharia, Ali would not have been driven to fight all those terrible battles against his own followers, who stood against him after the battle of 'Safeen', otherwise known as 'Al-Khawaarij', a word denoting dissent and opposition. If Sharia allows for political parties, or at least accepts the right to organise an opposing opinion, the Safeen battle itself would not have happened, the rivers of blood would not have run, and the companions of the Prophet would not have killed each other. Moreover, the famous 'Saqifah' allegiance would have been more democratic; there would have been no requirement for compulsory obedience to the appointed Caliph. Abu Bakr would not have appointed Omer as his successor; and Omer would not have restricted the 'Shoora'/'choice' to six people, with the power to kill any of the six if he refused to accept the proposed Caliph.

There is no doubt that Islamic Sharia texts, as currently understood and applied without going deep into their original meanings, i.e. their 'Taweel', deny the freedom of religion and freedom of thought. Moreover, they stipulate 'Jizya', or obligatory monetary punishment on Jews and Christians, and force them to pay it *'unwillingly, and in submission and humiliation'*, (Al-Touba: 29), rendering them as inferior and despicable people! Furthermore, a Muslim is not allowed to change her or his religion. If s/he does, s/he is to be killed for apostasy, as provided for in the Sudanese penal code today, in the first quarter of the 21st century. It is sufficient to say that Ustadh Mahmoud Mohammed Taha, the timeless teacher of generations, was executed on the basis of Islamic Sharia's apostasy law.

Regarding the International Covenant on Economic, Social and Cultural Rights, it provides for the right to social insurance, appropriate housing and clothing, freedom from hunger, healthcare, free education, participation in cultural life and creative activity, scientific research and equality between men and women. Other treaties and special agreements also deal comprehensively with matters relating to the elimination of all forms of discrimination, especially discrimination against women. We have previously shown that Islamic Sharia discriminates against women in obvious ways. This is why countries that adopt Sharia law have a lot of reservations on some provisions of these treaties and protocols.

Coming back to the Universal Declaration of Human Rights. The Declaration contains 30 articles establishing the constitutional principles that humanity has struggled for and dreamed of throughout the centuries. Article 4 of the Declaration prohibits slavery, and Article 5 prohibits torture, cruel, inhumane and degrading treatment. Article 16 establishes equality between men and women in marriage rights and Article 18 provides every person with the right to freedom of thought, conscience and religion, including the right to change one's religion or belief; Article 19 provides for freedom of expression and opinion. The remaining articles protect individual rights in a free society.

Considering all this, one can easily see that a religious government that applies Islamic Sharia, wherever and however it exists, is bound to forego and deny the provisions of the Universal Declaration of Human Rights at all times. It is inevitable, therefore, that any application of Sharia Law would go against the ascending march of humanity towards freedom and a better future.

The Stages of Constitutional Development in Sudan

The English colonial government that ruled Sudan (1899-1956) pursuant to the Anglo-Egyptian Rule Agreement, established the basic building blocks for the constitution and the rule of law in Sudan. Unfortunately, the consecutive national governments of Sudan have dissipated and neglected this great heritage, instead of safeguarding, maintaining and developing it. At the onset of the 20th century, the English government of Sudan issued various refined and civil legislations in harmony with legal principles that prevailed in England. Many of these laws followed the example of how those principles were administered in other colonies, especially in India. The Civil Justice Ordinance, the Penal Code, the Criminal Procedure Law, the Companies Act, the Land Settlement and Registration Act, etc. were all enacted. Towards the end of the 1940s, the Advisory Council of Northern Sudan was established and a legislative assembly was formed. In 1953, the Self-Government Statute was issued and was later developed into the Sudan Transitional Constitution 1956, the year of Sudan's independence from Britain and Egypt.

The 1956 constitution was one of the best constitutions in Sudan. It provided for fundamental rights for citizens without discrimination based on religion, belief or ethnicity, and it established freedom of expression and association. It also provided for the separation of powers, empowering the Supreme Court to act as interpreter/expounder and custodian of the constitution.

Unfortunately, this constitution was suspended in accordance with the Constitutional Order 1958 as a result of a military coup in the same year. At this point Sudan started to move timidly and hesitantly along a dark tunnel. Every attempt to move out of that tunnel has since then somehow caused the country to come back again to an even darker corner inside the same tunnel.

The 1956 constitution was revived through the birth of the 1964 Transitional Amended Constitution, as a result of a popular revolution, which overthrew military rule in October 1964. Because of this blessed uprising, Sudan was able to return to constitutionalism, legitimacy and the rule of law. However, it did not take long before the banners of the October revolution relapsed. The sectarian parties decided to amend article 5 (2) of the 1964 constitution, which read: 'Every person has a right to free expression of their views, and the right to form associations and unions in accordance with the law'. Pursuant to amending this pivotal article, the foundations of democratic rule collapsed and members of parliament representing 'graduate' constituencies were expelled from the Constituent Assembly.

Also, the Sudan Communist Party was disbanded. Moreover, the executive government refused to enforce a Supreme Court order, which decreed the dissolution of the Communist Party to be unconstitutional. The government announced that the Supreme Court's decision was only 'declaratory'. Therefore, the Supreme Court, the custodian of the constitution, was degraded and insulted and Sudan was returned to that dark tunnel again.

In May 1969 another military coup took place. Following a number of massacres, the 1973 constitution was issued. Naturally, there is no need to explain the content of that constitution, because one cannot really find a constitution under a totalitarian regime. The May coup continued to act in confusion, until Islamic Sharia was introduced in September 1983 (otherwise referred to as the September laws). Since that date, Sharia became the official state law, and all degrading and inhumane punishments were applied, and the country was firmly placed into the dark tunnel. This time the tunnel was totally and tightly closed. For this reason, the April 1985 popular uprising was unable to repeal the detestable September laws, because the collective mind of the people of Sudan was caught up in desperation, limitation and collapse.

Thus, it was convenient and easy for traditional and religious forces to seize power again through a military coup in June 1989. This coup was based on the arrangement, organisation, planning, conspiracy and deceit of the Muslim Brotherhood movement. This inauspicious coup declared the so-called 'Civilised Project' based on the rule of Islamic Sharia. From this point on, Sudan was clouded in a thick shadow of injustice, corruption, tyranny and carelessness with regards to the rule of law and individual rights. Political parties were disbanded, women forced to wear hijab, Jihad was declared against the non-Muslims of the South, and torture was inflicted on political opponents and crimes against humanity were committed. There is no need to discuss the 1998 constitution issued by the government of the Ingaz (Ingaz is Arabic for salvation, this is the name adopted by the ruling regime in Sudan), since the shadow cannot be straight when the rod is bent, and you cannot yield grapes out of thorns.

The Transitional Constitution of 2005 applied, or rather misapplied, by the Ingaz regime to govern the country during the transitional period, is dealt with in a separate article published in Arabic, titled: 'Let's allow reason to speak'. It is sufficient to say that this transitional constitution came into being as a result of the Comprehensive Peace Agreement (CPA). The CPA is a transitional agreement, which ended in 2011. No new constitution was made, and the transitional constitution has automatically become invalid. However, and for the sake of argument, if this transitional constitution is still valid, it is superseded by the CPA provisions. This is a bewildering situation, because the existence of a text that supersedes the text of the constitution creates a constitution devoid of meaning, even during the transitional period. The constitution is the fundamental and supreme law, and no other text should have any authority over it at any time.

In any event, the Ingaz government stands as a living example of the apparent contradiction between the idea of an Islamic government on the one hand, and the Holy Quran, the Sunnah, the constitution and the Universal Declaration of Human Rights on the other. The same applies to the rule of Taliban in certain areas of Afghanistan, which has tragically prohibited education for women; the same also applies to the terrorism of Hezbollah in Lebanon. It equally applies to the Shia'a government of Iraq as it inundates its country in a sea of blood in imitation of the Iranian model, which has delayed the clockwise motion of history, and threatened peace and security everywhere. Add to this, the 'Jihad' of Al-Qaeda, its terror and corruption in Syria and Yemen, and the Hamas government, which holds exclusive power in the Gaza Strip.

All these tragedies have not come about by mere chance. They are caused by the holding on to the fallacy and inherent error contained in the concept of an Islamic state. The result is contradictory, confused and violent policies. It makes no sense whatsoever. It is only reasonable to conclude that the concept of an Islamic government is totally false and is inherently erroneous however you approach it. Whatever is based on falsehood must be false. Nothing good could possibly come out of exploiting religion for political purposes.

THE FALLACY OF THE ISLAMIC STATE

Chapter
7

Spiritual Renaissance
and the Intellectual Revolution

In approaching the subject of the spiritual renaissance, it would be worthwhile for the reader to reflect deeply into this verse: *'when I evenly fashioned him, and breathed my spirit unto him, then prostrate in obeisance to him'* (Saad: 72). The expression: 'and breathed my spirit unto him' refers to the presence of the spirit of God eternally in the hearts of all human beings. The expression: 'when I evenly fashioned him' refers to the material formation of the human body, which is a continuous evolutionary process, because divine creativity is endless and inexhaustible. The even-fashioning and formation occurs at the mid-point of a pyramidal process, the base of which is physical existence and the top is the highest of heavens. This subtle meaning is reaffirmed in the verse: *'Thy who created, evenly fashioned, and perfectly rectified you'.* (Al-Infitaar: 7). In other words, the peak of physical even-fashioning embraces divine spirit, which is already breathed in the human form. Such equilibrium creates total harmony between matter and spirit.

Total holistic alignment of all images of existence, visible and invisible with spirit, is smoothly explained in these two verses: *'Thy who created, evenly fashioned and perfectly rectified you,* then shaped your image in every form of existence'* (Al-Infitaar: 7&8). The boundless ability of human beings to enter into all images of existence is a manifestation of divine spirit. This divine spirit breathed in the human being is eternally all pervading, enriching time and space.

'Thowra' is Arabic for Revolution. It means steadily and determinately moving upwards at ultimate speed. That is why the bull in Arabic is named 'Thowr'. The famous Arabic poet Bashar Ibn-Burd, used the same root of the word 'Thowra' to wonderfully describe a battle field scene:

> *Our swords were glittering, high above our heads*
> *Amidst the 'Mathar' of dust*
> *Like the night stars falling at dawn.*

This linguistic meaning is in harmony with the spiritual meaning hidden in the following two verses: *'fa-Atharna (raised up high) the dust * Dust as it accumulates and gathers at the mid-point'* (Al-A'diyat: 4&5). The even-fashioning of the human form rises up like dust, going up high in a revolutionary movement, to merge with God, through the breathing of the spirit, in harmony and rectitude. All is from God, as in the verse: *'All from Him'.* (Al-Gathiya: 13). All of this occurs at an extraordinary speed burning the sparks of the sacred fire in the dark night of the soul, until the sun of illumination has arisen. The Quran says *'The speeding steeps as they neigh* igniting sparks * raiding like fire at dawn'* (Al-A'adiyat:1, 2, 3).

The revolution of the intellect discussed here points to a deep-seated, holistic and radical transformation. It is a steady and powerful high leap, where all human beings emerge out of their limitation and rise up, abandoning the darkness of material formation, entering into the absoluteness of the light of spirit, thereby reaching out to the uppermost heights in a balanced evenness of illumination, without jeopardizing the sophisticated creation of the physical being. This balance is the essence of

'Taweel' of the Quran, which transcends all meaning without compromising the letter of the word. In other words the Taweel of the Quran gives words new and subtle meanings, not familiar or known in linguistic usage. However, this new meaning is still consistent and conforming with the literal meaning. This is confirmed by the Quran, as follows: *'Give full measure, when ye measure, and weigh with an accurate straight balance, that would be marvelous, and that is the best Taweel'* (Al-Isra': 35).

Let us meditate deeply upon these holy words of the Quran: *'Out of everything, we have created a pair, so ye may remember * Flee unto Allah, this is my clear warning to you'* (Al-Dhariyaat: 49&50). The expression: 'Out of everything we created a pair', refers to the conflict of opposites during the stage of even-fashioning of the physical body. Reflecting on that may trigger the remembrance of the spirit of God, which is always within us. When the light of God shines within ourselves, we remember 'home', whence we were in the kingdom of God, the age-old lost paradise. Then, we flee unto our Lord in a vertical inner movement, resembling a great leap. This inner movement is what we mean by the term intellectual revolution. The word 'flee' clearly indicates quick movement. The movement of the intellect is equally quick. It is in fact quicker than the speed of light. You may also notice this in your dreams.

If the mind stops swinging between the past and the future, it will become settled and more stable than mountains. As stated in the Quran: *'Allah will permanently settle the believers, by the eternal word, in this life and in the hereafter'* (Ibrahim: 27). In the good old days, Christ has also stated the same when he declared: 'Heaven and earth will pass away, but my words will never pass'. It goes without saying that Christ himself is the word of God, because his mind has been permanently settled in the present moment. The Quran addresses Mary, the mother of Jesus: *'God offers you glad tidings, a word from him, whose name is the Christ, Jesus the son of Mary'* (Al-Imraan: 45). What was possible and true for Christ could also be true for every human being. The Christ was only an example for the children of Israel, due to the full, complete and perfect grace bestowed on his mind by God. As the Quran reads: *'He-the Christ-is but a devotee, graced by Our blessings, and set as an example for the children of Israel'* (Al-Zukhruf: 59).

But the children of Israel, did not comprehend that Jesus is an example. That being that, they carry only the word, not the meaning of the Torah. The Quran describes this: *'Those who carried the words of the Torah but not the meanings, are like donkeys carrying books'* (Al-Juma'a: 5).

It is hoped that Muslims will learn the lesson, and not repeat the same mistake with the Quran, especially as there is a clear warning in the Quran pointing to this unfortunate destiny. The Quran reads: *'Is it not time for those who believe, that their hearts soften, upon the remembrance of Allah and the descendant truth? And not end up like those who were given the book before them, and they remained in darkness, deluded by time for so long, until their hearts were hardened'* (Al-Hadeed: 16).

In the same way, all the praiseworthy prophets were set as great examples, *'Those examples were set for the people, but only the knowledgeable would comprehend'* (Al-Ankabut: 43). This is perceived and appreciated by those who are present with God at all times and under all circumstances. The Quran says: *'The example of Jesus, and that of Adam are the same at the innermost abode of God'* (Al-Imran 59). Therefore, Jesus was a good word to set an example, as was Abraham and Mohamed and the rest of the prophets. All were marvelous words and examples of inspiration for realisation. They reflected the anticipation of receiving the treasures from the highest spirit, inside the heaven and earth of the self. *'He has the highest examples in the heaven and on the earth'.* (Al-Room: 27). However, in our heedlessness, we are not aware of that.

The Quran tells us: *'Don't you see? How God sets examples? A marvelous word is like a majestic tree, with roots deeply entrenched in the earth, and branches embracing the skies!'* (Ibrahim: 24). The latent meaning of the verse is that every human being is that 'marvelous word', rooted to and springing from the earth. That word has been created, evenly-fashioned in vertical rectitude reaching out to heavens, by the grace of the spirit of God breathed in all of us. The Quran exclaims: *'Within yourselves don't you have insight?'* (Al-Dhariyaat: 21). The intellectual revolution would have occurred for one who has this insight to perceive the spirit of God breathed in all of us. This is what we mean by the expression: 'the revolution of the intellect is individualistic'.

The Spirit is the well-nigh Static Consciousness. Even-Fashioning is the Dynamic Evolutionary Consciousness

Let us meditate upon these words of the Quran: *'Thy, is that who brought you forth from the same one Self, which is the well-neigh static (Mustagarr) as well as the dynamic evolutionary consciousness (Mustawda'a), we explained the signs for those who understand'* (Al-Ana'am: 98). The one self is the human self

131

that emerged from the grand presence of God, and manifested at different times and in various universes. From God it emerged and unto God it melts. This is the meaning of the Quranic expression in this verse: *'We belong to God and to Him we return'* (Al-Bagara: 156).

In the human self, there is a well-neigh static consciousness, referred to in the Quran thus: *'I breathed unto him of my spirit'.* Similarly, there is a dynamic evolutionary consciousness referred to by the Quranic expression *'When I evenly-fashioned him'.* Let us now explain what we mean by the term 'well-nigh static consciousness' and also the term 'dynamic evolutionary consciousness'.

Well-nigh Static Consciousness (Al-Mustaqarr)

The linguistic meaning for the Arabic word, 'Al-Mustaqarr', is derived from the Arabic root verb, Qarr, which means settled and stable. The spiritual and subtle meaning of Al-Mustaqarr refers to that immovable, static and silent consciousness, where everything ends. It means to settle in tranquility and relax in your being in silence. Nothing has to move, since there is no other place to move to. God is totally present in everything as everything, and is ever well-neigh static. Read the Quran here: *'On that day, unto your Lord is the ending (Al-Mustagarr) of the all'* (Al-Qiyaama: 12).

However, we do not feel the presence of Al-Mustaqarr within us. Not only this, but we do not recognise the presence of God's spirit breathed unto us. We are only aware of the presence of God within us, when we are consciously mindful of the present moment, a settled and perpetual timeless existence. The Quran says, addressing Moses: *'Look at the mountain, if it stays well-*

neigh static *(Istaqarra), you will see Me'*. (Al-A'raaf: 143). The word mountain is used here as a metaphor for the mind. Our minds settle in the present moment due to the vivid and silent act of the spirit of God that is deeply rooted in us. The Quran confirms in another verse: '*When he saw that it was well-neigh static within him (Mustaqirran), he declared: This is the remnant of my Lord'*(An-Naml: 40). The remnant of the Lord refers to the spirit of God breathed unto us. This has been re-iterated in the Quran as follows: '*The remnant of God is good for you if you believe, and I am not your keeper'* (Hood: 86).

All hope is hidden in this Quranic expression: 'I am not your keeper'. This expression refers to the lifting of the prophetical veil of custodianship over the believers. The believer has to stand alone, with a clear mind and a pure heart. Here, the search for God becomes the individual's responsibility, which is independent from Prophet Mohammed. Each person will now rely only on the spirit of God breathed unto him. This shining spirit of God inside us is not eclipsed by the dim darkness, gathered during the long and tiring physical earthly even-fashioning and formation. This subtle meaning is re-iterated in the Quranic verse: '*We knew that they never decrease, even beneath the earth, as the book is forever preserved'* (Quaaf: 4).

The same meaning is confirmed in the Quranic expression: '*We brought down the remembrance of truth (the Quran), and we are its preserving keeper'* (Al-Hijr: 9). The question to be asked is: where is the remembrance preserved? It is kept and stored in the chests of the knowers of truth, as stated in the Quran: '*It is clear signs within the chests of the knowers of truth'* (Al-Ankabut: 49).

Let us meditate upon the subtle knowledge cited above. Strangely enough, the righteous meditator will find all the verses of the Quran preserved in the highest place within his heart. Only righteous meditators are capable of this insight. This is confirmed in these verses: *'No! The book of the purely righteous is in the highest place* Are you aware of the meaning of the highest place? * It is an encrypted book * Only those closest to God, can witness'* (Al-Mutaffifeen: 18, 19, 20, 21).

This well-neigh static place is the highest place, *'And we raised him to the highest place'* (Mariam: 57). The highest place refers to the upward movement towards spiritual illumination. The Quran says: *'And make remembrance of Mary (Mariam in Arabic) in the book, as she withdrew from her people towards an Eastern place* When she veiled herself away from her people, we sent unto her our spirit, manifested perfectly as an evenly-fashioned human being'* (Mariam: 16 & 17).

The expression 'evenly-fashioned human being' refers to the perfection of a human being when they attain the highest place. At those heights, there is no swinging in the mind between past and present, due to the perfection and accuracy of the even-fashioning. The Quran refers to the time of this perfection thus: *'A Tryst that cannot be broken by neither of us; It is the 'even' place'* (Taha; 58).

In Taweel, the name 'Mary' points to the virgin pure self, which is the manifestation of spirit. However, we are not aware of this pure state of mind, due to our lack of knowledge. The Quran says: *'When they ask you about the spirit, answer them saying: the spirit is from the order of my Lord, you have been given but little knowledge'* (Al-Isra': 85). Our knowledge is little and scantly because of the limitation of the physical body and the shield of the five senses, which restrain the mind, thereby concealing the spirit, *'And she veiled herself away from her people'.* 'From her people' refers to her five senses.

It is a glad tiding that this veil will be lifted with the increase of our knowledge, by the grace of the light of spirit thrown into our mind, as it sees the truth. This is God's order. The Quran says: *'He imbues the spirit of His order upon whoever He wills'* (Ghaafir: 15). The spirit is the order of God as clearly expressed in this verse, and the previously mentioned verse, which reads: *'The spirit is from the order of my Lord'.*

The order of God is causeless. It is not influenced by external factors, or affected by anything outside itself. Everything exists within it. On the other hand, God's creation is His system, which depends on a causation that appears as if it is inherent within it. The Quran says: *'To Him belongs both order and creation, blessed is Allah, the Lord of everything'* (Al-A'araaf: 54). The merging of the world of order with the world of creation is the subject of religion. It is also the subject of the intellectual revolution.

This merging is a continuous meeting of these two worlds, through inspiration and awareness. It does not depend on reading books or repeating words. The Quran reads: *'Thus we have revealed to you the spirit of our order (highest order) as you were not aware of the meaning of the book or the meaning of belief... It is (book and belief) manifested as a light, through which we guide whom we ever wish)'* (Shoora: 52).

The lights of insight are permanently bright, abundant and uninterrupted. This divine status is confirmed in this Quranic verse *'Be Godly by that, which you have learned from the book, and by that which you have studied'* (Al-Imraan: 97). Learning and keeping the words of the book by heart, is an introduction to the study of the book. Studying of the book is the Taweel of the book, by going beyond words, and crossing over to the holy of holiness. The Arabic word for study *'dars'*, literally means 'crushing to the finest form, to extinction'. Learning and studying of the book (Quran) is the very essence of Taweel, which is elaborated in further detail in our other publications.

Another reason for our ignorance of the spirit, is that when the 'virgin self' is filled with the spirit, the light shines beyond the limitations of the brain. The Quran says with respect to the Virgin Mary (Mariam): *'She carried him, and withdrew with him to a remote place'* (Mariam: 22). This remote place is the furthest end in the city of knowledge, where all the knowledge of all the sages is the same, due to the oneness of the source of that knowledge. *'From the furthest end of the city, a man came walking, and he said: "Oh my people, follow the messengers"* (Yassin: 20). This verse instructs us to follow the essence of the messages of all the messengers. One should not follow the outer appearance. The essence is one, while manifestations vary.

Whoever reaches these lofty heights of spirit, God will empower and establish him/her with firm roots in the earth of the spirit. *'When they ask you about Zi Al-Gharneen, say: I will narrate his story to you * We empowered him on the earth (of the spirit) and taught him the causation of everything'* (Al-Kahf: 83, 84). Zi Al-Gharneen in Arabic literally means 'one with two horns'. It is a metaphor for every human being. In every human being, there is one horn pointing to the spirit, which is the well-neigh static consciousness, free from causation. The other horn points to the dynamic evolutionary consciousness. Empowerment on earth is possible to everyone who is contented with God, and in return, God is contented with him/her. *'He will empower them in their religion, which God is contented with'* (Al-Noor: 55). Contentment is the foundation of religion: *'He that lays the foundation of his edifice on purity, and contentment with God'* (Al-Touba: 109). Empowerment on earth was the lot of the chosen few of prophets and knowers of truth. Hopefully, it will be the lot and destiny of all human beings by the grace and will of God. The Quran states: *'It is Our will to shower Our grace on the downtrodden on earth, and make them leaders and inheritors * And to empower them on the earth'* (Al-Quasas: 5&6).

Empowerment on earth means that the heavens come down and have a place on earth, or rather that the earth rises up to a higher place where it becomes heaven. The earth will not attain this lofty status unless its inhabitants learn the word of God, and rise up to proficiently grasp the meaning of the words of Quran (Taweel). This is exactly what happened to Joseph the Prophet. The Quran says: *'Thus, We empowered Joseph on the earth by teaching him the Taweel of the words'* (Yousif: 21).

What was true for Joseph could be true for all the perfect ones. However, most people are not aware of that, as was clearly expressed in the previous verse, and confirmed in the immediately subsequent verse, which reads: *'Thus, We empowered Joseph on earth, by teaching him the Taweel of the words, and the highest order of God shall prevail, but most people know it not * When Joseph attained his full power, we granted him knowledge and high order; thus the perfect ones are rewarded'* (Yousif: 21&22).

Knowledge of 'Taweel' was the reason for the immediate appointment of Joseph as a trustee for the king, when the latter heard the Taweel of the words from Joseph. *'When he (Joseph) spoke to him (The king), the king said: Today you are empowered and entrusted'* (Yousif: 54). *The* word 'king' refers to the king of Egypt at the outer level (Tafseer). In the inner level, (Taweel), it refers to God, the king of kings. At this inner stage of consciousness, the self becomes aware of its own poverty and illusions. The Quran says: *'Today, the self owns nothing, and everything returns to God's order and ownership'* (Al-Infitaar: 19). 'Today' refers to the day of certitude, when the self becomes aware that God is the King of kings. Here, Taweel is the true Kingdom of God, for all knowers of truth. The Quran reads: *'Oh my Lord, You granted me the kingdom and taught me the Taweel of the words'* (Yousif: 101).

What remains to be said, is that Prophet Mohammed spoke the words of the Quran at a level where he was firmly established in the kingdom of his heart. The Quran reads: *'It is (The Quran), the words of a Nobel messenger * Empowered by the King of the Throne'* (Al-Takweer: 19 &20). The Arabic word for empowerment, 'Tamkeen', is derived from the root verb, 'Makkan', i.e. 'firmly established in a fortified manner'. The Arabic word, 'Makaan', which means 'space' is derived from the verb 'Kana', which means 'to be'. The Arabic word for universe is 'Koan'; whoever has a Koan, in heavens, also has a Makkan, or space on earth, i.e. empowered on earth. A Sudanese proverb describes a sage by this saying: 'He has a pillar in the sky, and a root in the earth'.

Based on this understanding, empowerment (Tamkeen) on earth is a spiritual term. It does not refer to a group of people, who take over political power and share public office and wealth amongst themselves without regard to competence or the principles of equality. Unfortunately, this word 'Tamkeen' has been used or rather 'misused' by Islamists to justify the false claim for the Islamic state.

The Dynamic Evolutionary Consciousness (Al-Mustawda'a)

The Arabic word, 'Al-Mustawda'a', means a storage place, or the place where an embryo is kept inside the body (the womb). This linguistic meaning is marvelous and in total harmony with the spiritual meaning of this word. Spiritually speaking, Al-Mustawda'a refers to the human brain, where all memory is stored. It is a dynamic storage, where information is constantly moving, adding and subtracting through remembrance and forgetfulness. In other words, Al-Mustawda'a refers to human consciousness, which acts as a container for memories.

The human brain is the storage of all memories and information, both inherited and acquired during one's life span. It is one brain, but each of us has a copy of it. The brain is open towards that which is well-neigh static (Al-Mustaqarr), and contains that which is dynamic (Al-Mustawda'a).

'Thy, is that who brought you forth from the same one Self; it is well-neigh static (Mustaqarr), and is evolutionary dynamic (Mustawda'a)' (Al-Ana'am: 98). This one self contains the human brain, where duality is created and is found in all human beings. The Quran says: *'Oh mankind, attain the purity of your Lord, who created you from one self, and from that self, he created its pair; and from the pair, he spread out many men and women; so attain the purity of Allah, whom you are demanding in the wombs, Allah is everlastingly observing you'* (Al-Nisaa: 1). The word 'womb' refers to Al-Mustawda'a, which in Arabic also means womb, as explained above.

The reader may have noticed that the word 'purity' was mentioned twice in this verse. Firstly purity refers to the purification of the Al-Mustawda'a (the human brain), which was referred to by the word 'wombs'. Secondly, purity also points to everlasting stillness in the Al-Mustagarr through constant observation of the movement of the human brain, which was referred to by the word 'Allah'.

What Do we Purify the 'Al-Mustawd'a' From?

The human brain (Al-Mustawda'a) contains our memories and our life story from birth to death. Our life story is the story of the conflict of opposites, both potential and kinetic. It is the conflict between what we project on actuality (what is), and imagine as good or evil, true or false, etc. This long and bitter conflict divided the human self, and created a state of contradiction in us. This state of contradiction is the reason for crimes and hostility amongst individuals and wars between nations.

The external conflict is just an apparent manifestation, resulting from internal contradictions stored in the human brain. If this contradiction is not resolved, anxiety and agitation will continue internally as well as externally. Therefore, it is the utmost responsibility of each individual to purify her/his storage (Al-Mustawda'a). This process of purification is what we call the revolution of the intellect.

If the above-mentioned is fully understood and absorbed, the revolution of the intellect would have already prevailed, and the contradiction between thought and actuality will come to an end. In this sense, the will of God is accomplished. The revolution of the intellect is the will of God that will never be defeated. The will of God is to purify the Mustawda'a. The Quran confirms:

'Allah only desires to remove impurity away from you Oh family of the House and to purify you again and again' (Al-Ahzaab: 33). 'The House' refers to the house of illumination, and 'family' refers to the knowers of truth, who attain the high status (Al-Mustaqarr). Notwithstanding their creed, colour, nationality or time, they are the knowers of truth, to whom Prophet Mohammed refers in the Quran thus: *'Oh my people, act from your place. I am acting from my place. Thus you will know'* (Al-Zumar: 39). In other words, act now, as I am acting now. This is the will of God, and you will realise that the will of God is pure goodness. Slowly read the Quran as it declares: *'No! you will know * No!, then you will know * No! you will know with certitude'* (Al-Takaathur: 3,4,5). This is certainly the true knowledge of the knowers of truth, who glorify God as Mohammed did. The Quran says: *'This is the truth of certitude * So, glorify the name of your Supreme Lord'* (Al-Wagia'a: 95, 96).

This realisation of truth with certitude leads to total freedom. This knowledge is the fuel of the revolution of the intellect, which will lead to total emancipation from rituals and from infatuation by personalities. This knowledge transforms you and me. You will see yourself as yourself where you are, and I will see myself as myself where I am, and Mohammed was already Mohammed where he was. Recite again this verse: *'Oh my people, act from your place. I am acting from my place. Thus you will know'.*

The Arabic word (Makanatakum), which means 'your place" was repeated four times in the Quran, (twice in Surah Hud, once in Surah Al-Anaam and once in Surah Al-Zummar). The number '4' has a spiritual significance, because it refers to the fourth dimension, which is the endless illumination of Godhood. For every word of the Quran, there are four layers of meaning. The first layer is external, the second layer is internal, the third is the realisation of truth, and the fourth one is the uninterrupted witnessing and living of the truth. In-between each layer of these meanings, there are endless signs of subtle meanings. The Quran says: *'We will show them our signs on the horizon and within themselves, till they clearly realise that it is the truth, was it not sufficient that your Lord is the witness of everything'* (Fussilat: 53).

The continuation of the conflict in the brain (Al-Mustawda'a) is our worst enemy. Outside enemies are mere illusions. Prophet Mohammed said: 'Your worst enemy is your very self'. The conflict inside the brain will not cool down, unless we attain our inner peace. Inner peace is the true heaven. Setting our thoughts pure and straight is the correct definition of paradise as apparent in the verse: *'He will guide them, and set their thoughts pure and straightened up* And admit them into paradise, the meaning of which He had revealed'* (Mohammed: 5&6).

Therefore, it is your responsibility to guide yourself on the straight path; and it is my responsibility to do the same. In true Islam there is no authoritative guardianship. No one has a right to judge the validity of another's belief. This is confirmed in the Quran addressing the believers thus: *'Oh believers: Your responsibility is strictly limited to yourself. Those who go astray cannot harm you, if you stay guided'* (Al-Ma'ida: 105).

However great and complex the conflict in the brain (Al-Mustawda'a) is, the well-neigh static consciousness remains quiet and still. It is not moved by the agitation of outside events. This timeless state of mind is not provoked by whatever happens outside. The Quran states: *'They told lies, and followed their whims, but the order of things remains well-neigh static (Mustaqirr)'* (Al-Gamar: 3).

The sun of truth ever shining in the present moment remains ever well-nigh static in the heart of every human being. The Quran says: *'The sun moves towards its well-neigh static destiny; that is the order of the All Exalted and the All Knowing'* (Yassin: 38). On the other hand, the physical sun is moving around its own orbit. Never still. Never reaching a destination, until it vanishes and fades away at the moment of its death. That is why Prophet Mohammed read the same verse above in a different manner to reflect this: *'The sun moves with no well-nigh static (Mustaqarr) destiny for it'.*

Ibn Abbas, one of Prophet Mohammed's companions, was aware of the two readings of this verse. Ibn Abbas acquired an introductory knowledge of Taweel. This was possible by the grace of Prophet Mohammed's prayer: 'May the Lord enable Ibn Abbas to understand religion, and know the Taweel'.

The full understanding of this well-nigh static consciousness, where all events of life take place, is the realisation of the intellectual revolution. Whoever is not aware of that, shall one day realise it. The Sufi poet says:

Do not rush into that, which you do not know,
You will only know, when you go slow

Read and reread the words of God, *'For every event, there is a well-neigh static consciousness (Mustagarr), and you will know'* (Al-Ana'am: 67). This well-neigh static consciousness (Almustaqarr), and the dynamic evolutionary consciousness (Al-Mustawda'a) are mentioned in another verse: *'He who knows its well-neigh static consciousness (its Mustaqarr), and its evolutionary dynamic consciousness (its Mustawda'a); All is written in the book of illumination'* (Hood: 6). The book of illumination refers to the Quran, and that is why the Taweel of Quran is significant for the intellectual revolution. Every human being is an end unto himself, because the well-neigh static consciousness (Al-Mustaqarr) rests within the human heart. Prophet Mohammed refers to Al-Mustaqarr, when he describes the attributes of God: 'My earth and my heaven did not contain Me. Only the heart of My faithful devotee contains Me'. Human knowledge stored in the brain (Al-Mustawda'a) increases every moment through enlightenment, *'Say oh my Lord, increase my knowledge'* (Taha: 114).

On the basis of the above, every human being is the seed of the ultimate perfect being. The Quran says: *'Everything is reckoned in a clarifying 'Imaam' (leader)'* (Yasin: 12). Therefore all hope rests on the individual human being. The human being is a sacred being. The appearance of the human form on earth means that the well-neigh static consciousness has touched the earth. The Quran says: *'You have on the earth a Mustaqarr (well-neigh static consciousness), and–for a while-a Mata'a (dynamic evolutionary consciousness)'* (Al-Bagara: 36, and also in Al-A'raaf: 24). Al-Mustaqarr, as previously explained, refers to God's spirit breathed within us. Mata'a is derived from the word Mustawda'a, i.e. that which is stored in the human brain. When the human brain is purified from the conflict of opposites, it will become meek, still, silent, pure and free from agitation. This purity allows for the spirit (Al-Mustaqarr) to merge with (Al-Mustawda'a) - in other words, God meeting with man. This is the true meaning of the intellectual revolution. This meaning is also highlighted in the bible, which reads: 'Blessed are the pure in the heart, for they see God', and 'Blessed are the poor in spirit, for theirs is the Kingdom of Heaven'.

This is the Revolution of the Intellect, which Exists in the Hearts of all Human Beings

Explaining the various aspects of the intellectual revolution can be creatively approached from various angles. It is an inner revolution that shines outwards. It does not need processions or demonstrations. It is pure peace.

All revolutions in the past have been an expression of human agitation and conflict. They exploded from the 'Al-Mustawda'a'. They were bloody expressions of the internal conflict in the human brain. All the revolutions of Al-Mustawda'a have been bloody, as happened in the American War of Independence and the French Revolution. However, the religious revolutions were more violent and superficial, for example the Iranian Revolution. The attempts by Iran to spread the Shia'a revolution through its followers in Iraq, Lebanon and Bahrain were also violent.

The revolution of the intellect is the only peaceful revolution, since it emerges from the well-neigh static consciousness (Al-Mustaqarr), where peace and tranquility reside. It will come without processions and demonstrations. It is the inner and spiritual revolution of Al-Mustaqarr.

The Quran will lead smoothly, easily and effortlessly to remembrance. As stated in this verse: *'The Quran leads easily to remembrance. Is there one to remember?'* (Al-Gamar: 17, 22, 32, 40). Note that this verse is repeated four times in the same Surah. Observation of the movement of the self will lead to tranquility. Through the remembrance of Allah, the heart rests in peace. In other words, remembrance will lead to Al-Mustaqarr. If one continues from moment to moment to remember and observe the movement of the self, Allah will lead him/her to Himself. The Quran says:

145

'Remember Me, I will remember you' (Al-Bagara: 152). Remembrance of Allah will automatically lead to purification of thought. The Quran says: *'Remembrance descended upon you (Mohammed), to show the people that, which was brought down to them, so they may think properly'* (Al-Nahl: 44).

The expression 'think properly' refers to purification of thought. Purification of thought is the essence of the intellectual revolution, where the dynamic evolutionary consciousness (Al-Mustawda'a) becomes one with the well-neigh static God consciousness. Here, religion ceases to be a dogma and a ritual, and human beings aspiration for peace could be realised.

Those who believe in the concept of the Islamic state are engaged in one of the most violent, bloody and dangerous Mustawda'a revolutions. The aim of their revolution is to impose their own 'Mustawda'a' ideas on others, using the false concept of an Islamic state. Therefore, nothing good could come out of it. Moreover, this false concept of an Islamic state is a real threat to world peace and security, and could ultimately lead to the collapse of civilisation.

If this situation is left unchecked, Islam will become an impediment and a great obstacle standing in the way of human liberation and final redemption, and will represent a huge setback on the road to peace.

Renewal of Islam through the understanding of Taweel is inevitable and is an urgent necessity. This understanding will reveal the true knowledge of the well-neigh static consciousness (Al-Mustaqarr), where the sun of truth is eternally shining in the caves of our hearts.

www.ingramcontent.com/pod-product-compliance
Lightning Source LLC
LaVergne TN
LVHW011241080426
835509LV00005B/580